INSPIRE
MATHS

C000212947

PUPIL TEXTBOOK
3B

Noogol

Googol

Koogol

Ooogol

Toogol

Zoogol

Consultant and author
Dr Fong Ho Kheong
Authors
Chelvi Ramakrishnan and Michelle Choo
UK consultants
Carole Skinner, Simon d'Angelo and Elizabeth Gibbs

Introduction

Inspire Maths is a comprehensive, activity-based programme designed to provide pupils with a firm foundation in maths and to develop the creative and critical thinking skills to become fluent problem solvers.

Inspire Maths makes learning maths fun and rewarding through the use of engaging illustrations and games that help to reinforce and consolidate learning.

For the teacher:

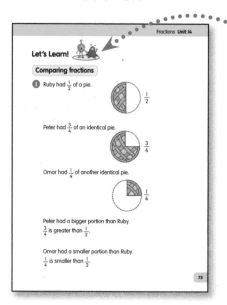

Use the engaging and highly scaffolded **Let's Learn!** to introduce concepts. Integrated questions allow for immediate assessment and consolidation of concepts learnt.

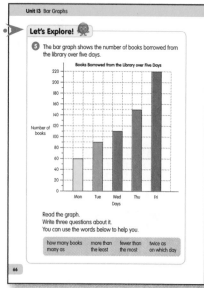

Carry out investigative activities in **Let's Explore!** These allow pupils to apply concepts learnt.

Challenge pupils to solve non-routine questions by applying relevant heuristics and thinking skills in **Put On Your Thinking Caps!**

For the parent/guardian:

Build home-school links and make maths come alive by using the tips in Home Maths to help children apply mathematical concepts to daily life.

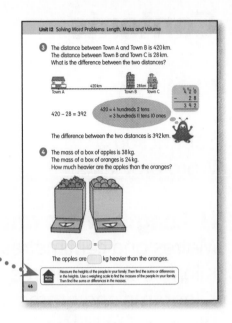

For the pupil:

Enjoy **Inspire Maths** with your friends. Explore your learning through activities and games.

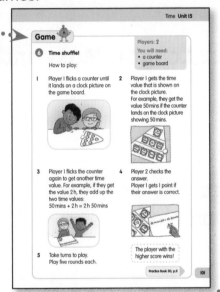

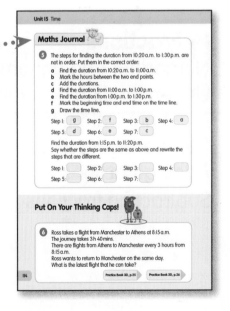

Share what you have learnt, create your own questions and become aware of your own mathematical thinking in your Maths Journal.

Contents

Let's Learn!

Addition

1 Ella bought some cheese for £5·35.
She also bought a bag of apples for £2·00.
How much did Ella spend altogether?

£5·35

£2·00

+

£5·35 + £2·00 = ?

Ella spent £7·35 altogether.

First add the pounds.

£5 + £2 → £7

Then add the pence.

£7 + 35p → £7·35

2 Add the pounds.
Then add the pence.

   a £2·15 + £7·00   **b** £5·00 + £3·75

3 Farha bought a banana for £0·55.
She also bought a box of cereal for £3·20.
How much did Farha spend altogether?

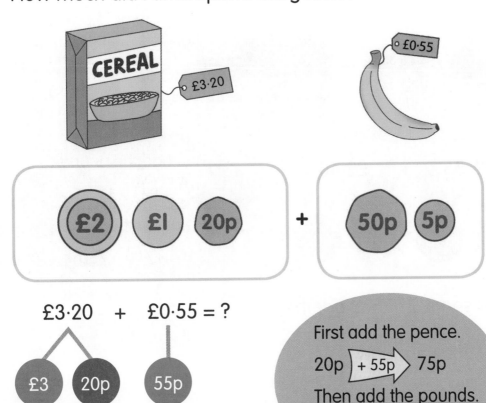

£3·20 + £0·55 = ?

First add the pence.

20p + 55p ⟶ 75p

Then add the pounds.

75p + £3 ⟶ £3·75

Farha spent £3·75 altogether.

4 Add the pence.
Then add the pounds.

  a   £0·45 + £4·25   **b**   £15·25 + £0·15

5 Add the pounds or the pence first.

  a   £6·45 + £4·00   **b**   £12·35 + £8·00

  c   £5·40 + £0·55   **d**   £3·25 + £0·65

6 Peter bought some cheese for £5·35.
He also bought a loaf of bread for £2·40.
How much did Peter spend altogether?

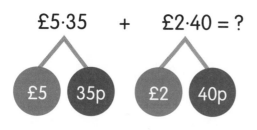

£5·35 + £2·40 = ?

£5 35p   £2 40p

Peter spent £7·75 altogether.

First add the pounds.

£5 + £2 → £7

Next add the pence.

35p + 40p → 75p

Then add 75p to £7.

£7 + 75p → £7·75

7 Ruby bought a DVD for £9·15.
She also bought a notebook for £3·85.
How much did Ruby spend altogether?

 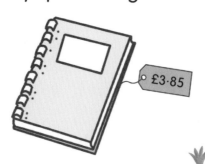

£9·15 + £3·85 = £12 + £1
            = £13

Ruby spent £13 altogether.

Add the pounds.
£9 + £3 = £12

Add the pence to
make one pound.
15p + 85p = £1

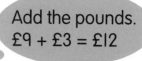

8 First add the pounds.
Then add the pence.
Finally add the pounds and pence.

    a £8·15 + £1·45   **b** £3·35 + £6·60

    c £21·15 + £7·75   **d** £5·45 + £18·35

9 Answer these questions.
Add the pence to make one pound first.

    a £6·45 + £3·55   **b** £7·35 + £8·65

    c £11·15 + £8·85   **d** £14·25 + £15·75

Practice Book 3C, p.7

10 A tennis racket costs £12·35.
A tube of tennis balls costs £4·95.
What is the total cost of the tennis racket and the
tube of tennis balls?

£12·35 + £4·95 = £12·30 + £5
                  = £17·30

Add the 5p to £4·95.
£4·95 + 5p = £5

£12·30   5p

The tennis racket and the tube of tennis balls cost £17·30.

11 Add mentally.

a £3·55 + £4·95 = £ ☐

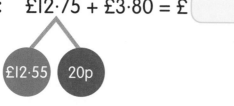

£3·50 **5p**

b £6·25 + £8·90 = £ ☐

£6·15 **10p**

c £12·75 + £3·80 = £ ☐

£12·55 **20p**

d £15·65 + £4·85 = £ ☐

£15·50 **15p**

12 A tub of ice cream costs £6·70.
A cereal bar costs £0·80.
What is the total cost of the ice cream and the cereal bar?

£6·70 + £0·80 = ?

£6·70 + £1 £7·70

£7·70 – 20p £7·50

Adding 80p is the same as adding £1 and subtracting 20p.

80p

20p

£1

The ice cream and the cereal bar cost £7·50.

13 Find the missing amounts.

a £4·80 + £0·90 = ?

£4·80 + ◯ £ ☐

£ ☐ – ◯ £ ☐

£4·80 + £0·90 = £ ☐

b £23·65 + £0·95 = ?

£23·65 + ◯ £ ☐

£ ☐ – ◯ £ ☐

£23·65 + £0·95 = £ ☐

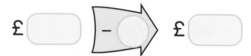

Practice Book 3C, p.9

14 £8·75 + £2·20 = ?

```
  £ 8 · 7 5
+ £ 2 · 2 0
───────────
```

This is another way of adding pounds and pence.

```
  8 7 5 p
+ 2 2 0 p
─────────
1 0 9 5 p
```

Adding pounds and pence is just like adding numbers.

```
  8 7 5
+ 2 2 0
───────
1 0 9 5
```

```
  £   8 · 7 5
+ £   2 · 2 0
─────────────
  £ 1 0 · 9 5
```

£8·75 + £2·20 = £10·95

15 £9·30 + £15·45 = ?

```
  £   9 · 3 0
+ £ 1 5 · 4 5
─────────────
```

```
+     [   ] p
    [   ] p
  ───────────
    [   ] p
```

```
      £ [   ]
+   £ [   ]
  ───────────
    £ [   ]
```

£9·30 + £15·45 = £ [   ]

16 Find the sum of £8·35 and £2·85.

Here is another way to add!

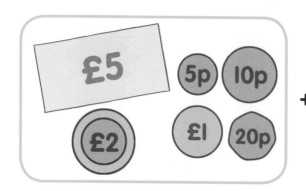

+

£8·35 + £2·85 = ?

First add the pence.

```
  £ 8 · 3 5
+ £ 2 · 8 5
  £     2 0
        ₁   ₁
```

Then add the pounds.

```
  £   8 · 3 5
+ £   2 · 8 5
  £ 1 1 · 2 0
      ₁     ₁
```

£8·35 + £2·85 = £11·20

Adding in this way is just like adding numbers.

```
    8 3 5
+   2 8 5
  1 1 2 0
    ₁   ₁
```

17 Add.

a
```
  £ 7 · 4 5
+ £ 9 · 7 5
  £ (     )
```

b
```
  £ 1 6 · 0 5
+ £ 2 8 · 9 5
  £ (      )
```

Home Maths

When you go shopping with your child, choose two items and ask them to find the total cost by adding mentally.

Activity

18 Look at the advertisement below.

SHOP

Packet of hair bands 60p

Batteries £3·85

cornflakes

Raincoat £16·70

Cornflakes £4·50

Comb £1·10

Mobile phone £85·40

Umbrella £9·30

Work with a partner to find the cost of:

a a packet of hair bands and a box of cornflakes.

b a mobile phone and a pack of batteries.

c two combs.

d a raincoat and an umbrella.

e a raincoat and mobile phone.

f two mobile phones.

Practice Book 3C, p.11

Let's Learn!

Subtraction

1 Ali has £18·95 in his wallet.
He buys a pair of shoes for £16·00.
How much money does Ali have left in his wallet?

£16·00

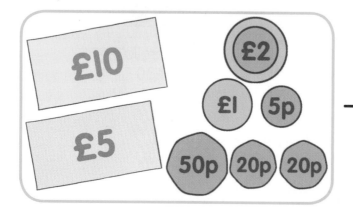

−

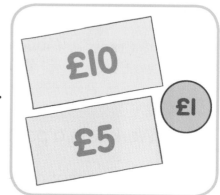

£18·95 − £16·00 = ?

£18 95p   £16

First subtract the pounds.

£18 − £16 ➔ £2

Then add the pence.

£2 + 95p ➔ £2·95

Ali has £2·95 left in his wallet.

2 Tai's mum has £28·95 in her purse.
After buying a top, she has £0·50 left in her purse.
How much does she pay for the top?

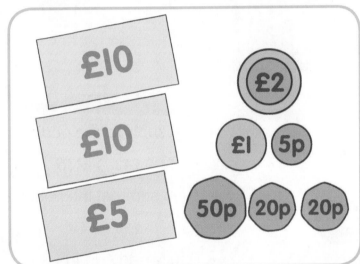

£28·95 – £0·50 = ?

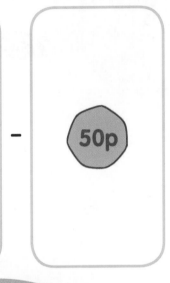

First subtract the pence.

95p – 50p → 45p

Then add 45p to £28.

£28 + 45p → £28·45

She pays £28·45 for the top.

3 Subtract.

a   £17·85 – £4·00

b   £15·45 – £8·00

c   £21·75 – £0·30

d   £23·95 – £0·70

4 Jack's dad buys a pair of trousers for £79·65.
He also buys a shirt for £43·25.
How much more does the pair of trousers cost than the shirt?

£79·65 – £43·25 = ?

£79   65p   £43   25p

First subtract the pounds.

£79 – £43   £36

Then subtract the pence.

65p – 25p   40p

Finally add 40p to £36.

£36 + 40p   £36·40

The pair of trousers costs £36·40
more than the shirt.

5 First subtract the pounds.
Then subtract the pence.
Finally add the pounds and pence.

  a   £65·75 – £12·45   **b**   £78·65 – £23·05

Practice Book 3C, p.13

6 A watermelon costs £4·70.
An apple costs £0·80.
How much less does the apple cost than the watermelon?

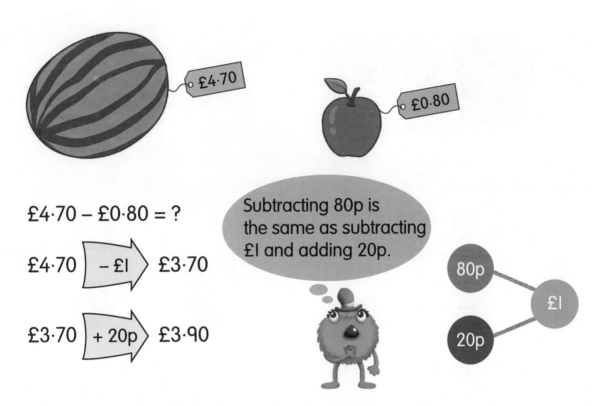

£4·70 − £0·80 = ?

£4·70 [− £1 ⟩ £3·70

Subtracting 80p is the same as subtracting £1 and adding 20p.

£3·70 [+ 20p ⟩ £3·90

The apple costs £3·90 less than the watermelon.

7 Find the missing amounts.

a £5·60 − £0·90 = ?

£5·60 [− ◯ ⟩ £ ☐

£ ☐ [+ ◯ ⟩ £ ☐

£5·60 − £0·90 = £ ☐

b £12·55 − £0·85 = ?

£12·55 [− ◯ ⟩ £ ☐

£ ☐ [+ ◯ ⟩ £ ☐

£12·55 − £0·85 = £ ☐

8 Hardeep has £9·70.
He buys a mug for £4·90.
How much does he have left?

£9·70 – £4·90 = ?

£9·70 – £5 £4·70

£4·70 + 10p £4·80

Hardeep has £4·80 left.

Subtracting £4·90 is the same as subtracting £5 and adding 10p.

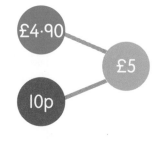

9 Find the missing amounts.

a £8·40 – £5·80 = ?

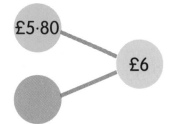

£8·40 – £5·80 = £ ⬚

b £15·45 – £8·95 = ?

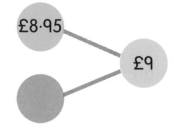

£15·45 – £8·95 = £ ⬚

Practice Book 3C, p.15

10 £9·65 – £4·30 = ?

$$\begin{array}{r} £\ 9\cdot6\ 5 \\ -\ £\ 4\cdot3\ 0 \\ \hline \end{array}$$

$$\begin{array}{r} 9\ 6\ 5\text{p} \\ -\ 4\ 3\ 0\text{p} \\ \hline 5\ 3\ 5\text{p} \end{array}$$

$$\begin{array}{r} £\ 9\cdot6\ 5 \\ -\ £\ 4\cdot3\ 0 \\ \hline £\ 5\cdot3\ 5 \end{array}$$

£9·65 – £4·30 = £5·35

This is another way of subtracting pounds and pence.

Subtracting pounds and pence is just like subtracting numbers.

$$\begin{array}{r} 9\ 6\ 5 \\ -\ 4\ 3\ 0 \\ \hline 5\ 3\ 5 \end{array}$$

11 £11·85 – £4·55 = ?

$$\begin{array}{r} £\ 1\ 1\cdot8\ 5 \\ -\ £\ \ \ 4\cdot5\ 5 \\ \hline \end{array}$$

$$\begin{array}{r} \boxed{}\text{p} \\ -\ \boxed{}\text{p} \\ \hline \boxed{}\text{p} \end{array}$$

$$\begin{array}{r} £\ \boxed{} \\ -\ £\ \boxed{} \\ \hline £\ \boxed{} \end{array}$$

£11·85 – £4·55 = £ $\boxed{}$

12 Find the difference between £27·30 and £15·40.

Here is another way to subtract!

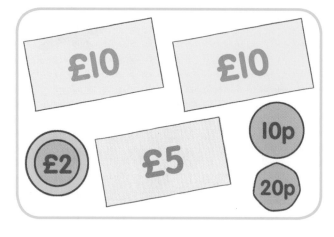

£27·30 – £15·40 = ?

First regroup £27·30.

£27·30 = £26 + 130p

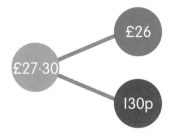

Then subtract the pence.

```
  £ 2 ⁶7̶ · ¹3 0
– £ 1 5 · 4 0
─────────────
  £       · 9 0
```

Subtracting in this way is just like subtracting numbers.

```
  2 ⁶7̶ ¹3 0
– 1 5 4 0
─────────
  1 1 9 0
```

Finally subtract the pounds.

```
  £ 2 ⁶7̶ · ¹3 0
– £ 1 5 · 4 0
─────────────
  £ 1 1 · 9 0
```

13 Subtract.

a

$$
\begin{array}{r}
£\ 1\ 8\ \cdot\ 3\ 0 \\
-\ £\ \ \ \ \ 2\ \cdot\ 4\ 0 \\
\hline
£\ \boxed{} \\
\hline
\end{array}
$$

Regroup.

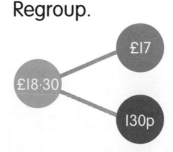

b

$$
\begin{array}{r}
£\ 2\ 5\ \cdot\ 0\ 0 \\
-\ £\ \ \ \ \ 7\ \cdot\ 8\ 5 \\
\hline
£\ \boxed{} \\
\hline
\end{array}
$$

Regroup.

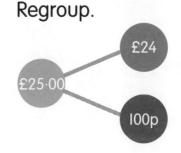

Practice Book 3C, p.17

Maths Journal

14 Peter made a mistake while subtracting.

$$
\begin{array}{r}
£1\ 5\ \cdot\ 2\ 5 \\
-\ £\ \ 8\ \cdot\ 4\ 0 \\
\hline
£\ \ 7\ \cdot\ 8\ 5 \\
\hline
\end{array}
$$

Did he make a mistake in subtracting the pence?
Did he make a mistake in subtracting the pounds?
Explain and write one or two lines about how he made
the mistake.

Millie made a mistake.

$$
\begin{array}{r}
£\ \ \ 9\ \cdot\ 4\ 5 \\
-\ £\ \ 7\ \cdot\ 3\ 0 \\
\hline
£1\ 6\ \cdot\ 7\ 5 \\
\hline
\end{array}
$$

Explain and write one or two lines about how she made
the mistake.

Let's Learn!

Word problems

1 Farha's dad has £35·50.
He buys a magazine and has £29·30 left.
How much does he spend on the magazine?

£35·50 − £29·30 = £6·20

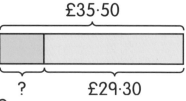

£35·50

? £29·30

Farha's dad spends £6·20 on the magazine.

2 Jack has £12 in his money box.
He buys a glass of orange juice for £2·50
and a DVD for £7·90.
How much money does he have left?

How much
money is left?

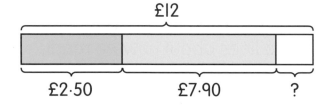

£12

£2·50 £7·90 ?

First find the amount of money Jack spends.
£2·50 + £7·90 = £10·40

Then subtract this amount from Jack's savings.
£12·00 − £10·40 = £1·60

Jack has £1·60 left.

3 Peter has £25·50.
Sarah has £18·75.

How much more money
does Peter have than Sarah?

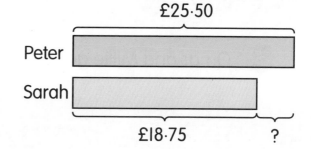

£ ⬭ – £ ⬭ = £ ⬭

Peter has £ ⬭ more than Sarah.

4 A jumper costs £24·85.
A T-shirt is £3·40 cheaper than the jumper.
How much do the jumper and the T-shirt cost altogether?

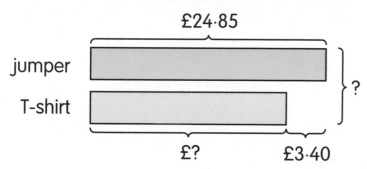

£ ⬭ ⬭ £ ⬭ = £ ⬭

The T-shirt costs £ ⬭ .

First find the cost
of the T-shirt.

£ ⬭ ⬭ £ ⬭ = £ ⬭

The jumper and the T-shirt cost £ ⬭ altogether.

Activity

5 Omar and Millie go to the museum.

Look at the picture above.
Then look at p25. Think of some questions and work out the answers.

Look at these examples.

Example

Omar and Millie buy two tickets.
Question: How much do the two tickets cost?
Answer: £7·50 + £7·50 = £15·00

A guidebook costs more than a badge.
Question: How much more does the
guidebook cost than the badge?
Answer: £3·20 − £1·50 = £1·70

Read sentences **a**, **b**, **c**, **d** and **e**.

Write a question for each sentence in your book and answer it.

a   Omar and Millie buy a keyring and a pencil.

Question:

Answer:

b   Omar buys a museum ticket and a badge.

Question:

Answer:

c   A pencil costs less than a keyring.

Question:

Answer:

d   A keyring costs more than a badge.

Question:

Answer:

e   Omar buys a museum ticket on Saturday for £9·50.

Question:

Answer:

Practice Book 3C,
p.19 and 21

Put On Your Thinking Caps!

6　**a**　Tai buys a hat and a scarf.
The total cost is £18.
The scarf cost £2 more than the hat.
How much does he spend on the hat?

scarf

hat

b　Miya buys some pencils and rubbers.
She spends £1·20 altogether.
The pencils cost £0·40 more than the rubbers.
How much does she spend on the rubbers?
Give your answers in pence.
(Use a model to solve this word problem.)

Practice Book 3C, p.25　　Practice Book 3C, p.26

Unit 11 — Length, Mass and Volume

Let's Learn!

Metres and centimetres

1 The length of the ribbon is 1 metre.

The **metre (m)** and **centimetre (cm)** are units of length.

100 cm

The ribbon is 100 times as long as 1 centimetre.
1 m = 100 cm

1 m

2 Millie's height is 1 m 38 cm.
What is her height in centimetres?

1 m 38 cm
- 1 m = 100 cm
- 38 cm

1 m 38 cm = 100 cm + 38 cm
= 138 cm

Millie's height is 138 cm.

27

3 The length of a room is 4 m 56 cm.
Find the length of the room in centimetres.

4 m 56 cm = ⬚ cm + ⬚ cm

= ⬚ cm

The length of the room is ⬚ cm.

4 m 56 cm ⟨ 4 m
         56 cm

4 Ruby jumps 125 cm from the starting line.
How many metres and centimetres does she jump?

125 cm

100 110 120 130

1 m 25 cm

125 cm ⟨ 100 cm = 1 m

         25 cm

125 cm = 100 cm + 25 cm

       = 1 m 25 cm

She jumps 1 m 25 cm.

5 The snake is ⬚ cm long.

It is ⬚ m ⬚ cm long.

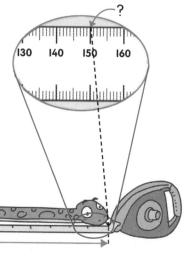

?

130 140 150 160

6 Complete the following:

3 m 75 cm

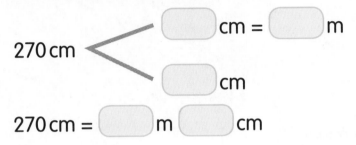

☐ m = ☐ cm

☐ cm

3 m 75 cm = ☐ cm

7 Complete the following:

270 cm

☐ cm = ☐ m

☐ cm

270 cm = ☐ m ☐ cm

Activity

8 You will need a tape measure and a bean bag.

1 Stand behind a starting line and throw the bean bag as far as you can.

2 Estimate how far the bean bag is from the starting line.

3 Measure the distance with the tape measure.

4 Copy the chart below. Write your estimate and your actual distance in the chart. Compare your measurements with your friends.

	My Estimate	My Measurement
Distance from Starting Line	☐ m ☐ cm	☐ m ☐ cm

Practice Book 3C, p.29

Let's Learn!

Kilometres and metres

1 The children measure the length of a football pitch to find out how long 1 kilometre is.

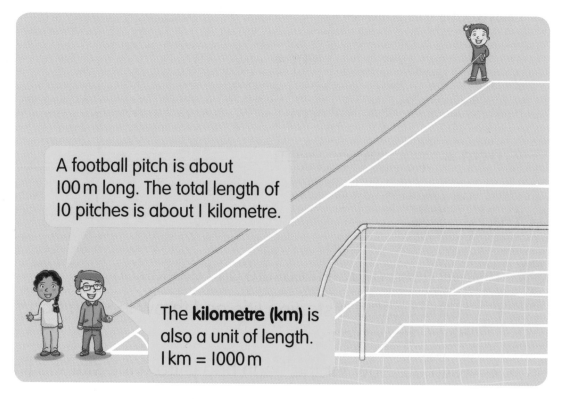

A football pitch is about 100 m long. The total length of 10 pitches is about 1 kilometre.

The **kilometre (km)** is also a unit of length.
1 km = 1000 m

2 We use kilometres to measure long distances.

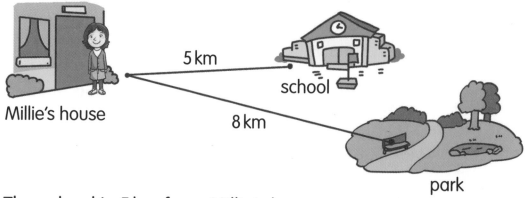

Millie's house

5 km

school

8 km

park

The school is 5 km from Millie's house.
The park is 8 km from Millie's house.

3 Peter lives in this house.

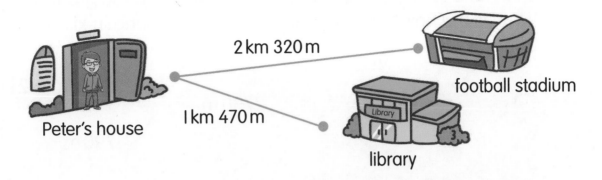

2 km 320 m

I km 470 m

football stadium

Peter's house

library

a The distance between the library and Peter's house is
I km 470 m.
What is the distance in metres?

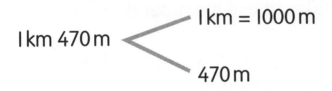

I km 470 m

I km = 1000 m

470 m

I km 470 m = 1000 m + 470 m
           = 1470 m

The distance is 1470 m.

b The football stadium is ⬚ km ⬚ m from Peter's house.

The distance between the football stadium and Peter's house is ⬚ m.

4 Jack is on a plane.
The plane is flying at a height of 2790 m above the ground.
What is the height of the plane above the ground in kilometres and metres?

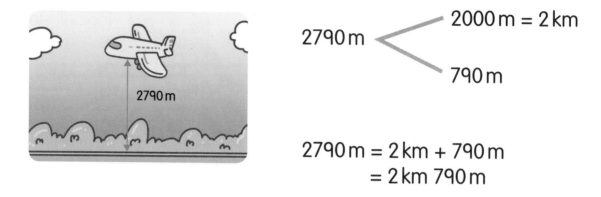

$2790 \text{ m} \big< \begin{array}{l} 2000 \text{ m} = 2 \text{ km} \\ 790 \text{ m} \end{array}$

$$2790 \text{ m} = 2 \text{ km} + 790 \text{ m}$$
$$= 2 \text{ km } 790 \text{ m}$$

The plane is 2 km 790 m above the ground.

5 The distance from Ben's house to school is 5275 m.
He cycles to school every morning.
What is the distance he cycles in kilometres and metres?

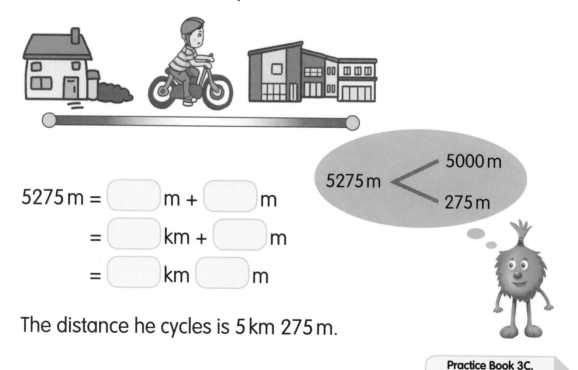

$5275 \text{ m} = \boxed{} \text{ m} + \boxed{} \text{ m}$

$\quad\quad = \boxed{} \text{ km} + \boxed{} \text{ m}$

$\quad\quad = \boxed{} \text{ km} \boxed{} \text{ m}$

$5275 \text{ m} \big< \begin{array}{l} 5000 \text{ m} \\ 275 \text{ m} \end{array}$

The distance he cycles is 5 km 275 m.

Practice Book 3C,
p.31 and 33

Let's Learn!

Kilograms and grams

1 The bunch of grapes has a mass of 1 kilogram.

The **kilogram (kg)** and **gram (g)** are units of mass.

1 kg = 1000 g

One small marking on this scale stands for 100 g.

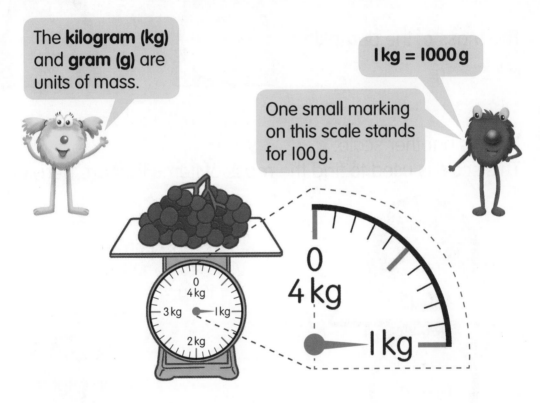

2 Here is another scale.
This scale is used to find the mass of items that are light.

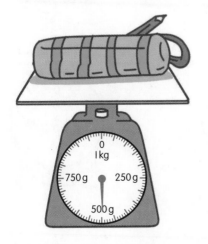

Use this scale to measure mass less than 1 kg.
One small marking stands for 10 g.

3 The carrots have a mass of 600 g.
What is the mass of the pumpkin?

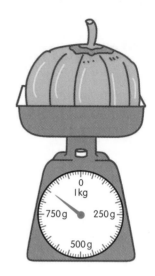

The mass of the pumpkin is ⬚ g.

4 Here is another scale.
This scale is used to find the mass of items that are heavier.

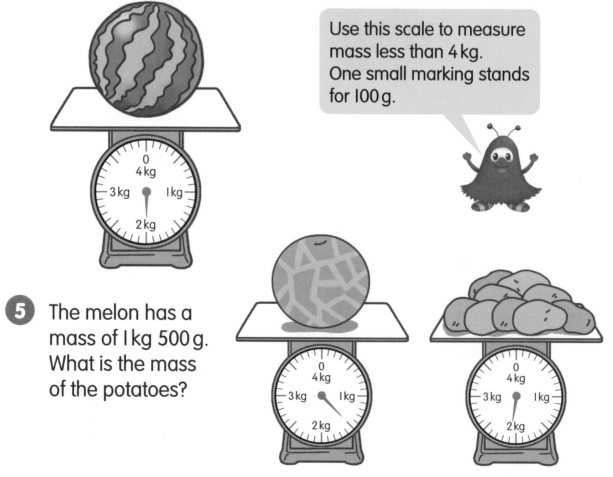

Use this scale to measure mass less than 4 kg.
One small marking stands for 100 g.

5 The melon has a mass of 1 kg 500 g.
What is the mass of the potatoes?

The mass of the potatoes is 2 kg 100 g.

6 Find the mass of each item.

Read the scales.

a

The mass of the apples
is ⬡ g.

b

The mass of the
cabbage is ⬡ g.

c

The mass of the
pineapples is ⬡ g.

d

The mass of the
melon is ⬡ g.

Activity

7 You will need these objects.

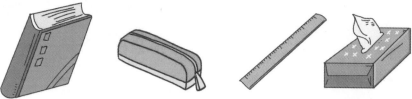

Work in groups of four.

I Estimate the mass of each object.

2 Find the mass of each object using a scale.

3 List them in a chart like the one below.

Object	My Estimate	Actual Mass
book	I kg 250 g	I kg 300 g

8 The mass of a bag of potatoes is I kg 250 g.
What is the mass of the bag of potatoes in grams?

I kg 250 g ⟨ I kg = 1000 g
                250 g

I kg 250 g = 1000 g + 250 g

= 1250 g

The mass of the bag of potatoes is 1250 g.

9 The mass of a bag of rice is 3450 g.
What is its mass in kilograms and grams?

3450 g
$3000\,g = 3\,kg$
$450\,g$

$3450\,g = 3000\,g + 450\,g$
$= 3\,kg\,450\,g$

The mass of the bag of rice is 3 kg 450 g.

10 Complete the following:

8 kg 405 g
$\boxed{}\,kg = \boxed{}\,g$
$\boxed{}\,g$

$8\,kg\,405\,g = \boxed{}\,g$

11 Complete the following:

5805 g
$\boxed{}\,g = \boxed{}\,kg$
$\boxed{}\,g$

$5805\,g = \boxed{}\,kg\,\boxed{}\,g$

12 Write the mass in grams.

a 6 kg 921 g   **b** 1 kg 78 g   **c** 9 kg 6 g

13 Write the mass in kilograms and grams.

a 3425 g   **b** 9059 g   **c** 8008 g

Practice Book 3C, p.35

Let's Learn!

Litres and millilitres

1 How much water can this bottle hold?

> The measuring jug is marked in **litres (ℓ)** and **millilitres (ml)**.

1 ℓ = 1000 ml

The **volume** of water in the bottle is 1 ℓ.
This bottle can hold up to 1 litre of water.
Its **capacity** is 1 ℓ.

> This is how much 1 ℓ is as compared to 10 ml.

Volume and capacity are measured in
litres and **millilitres**.

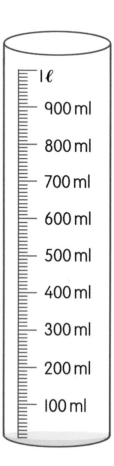

1 ℓ
900 ml
800 ml
700 ml
600 ml
500 ml
400 ml
300 ml
200 ml
100 ml

10 ml
5 ml

38

2 The flask has a capacity of 1 ℓ 400 ml.

$$1\,\ell = 1000\,ml$$
$$1\,\ell\ 400\,ml = 1000\,ml + 400\,ml$$
$$= 1400\,ml$$

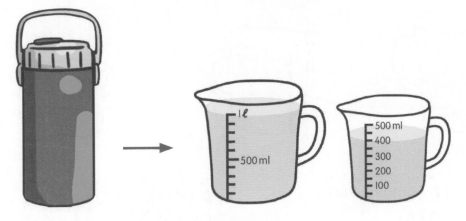

3 How is volume different from capacity?

Container A is partly filled with water.
Its volume is 800 ml.

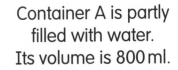

A

The amount of water in a container is called the **volume** of water.

Add water up to the brim.

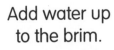

A

Container A is now completely filled with water.

The **capacity** of a container is the full amount of water it can hold.

Empty the water into measuring jugs.

The capacity of Container A is 1 ℓ 200 ml.

4 Ella has some measuring jugs.
Each measuring jug has different markings.
How much water does one small marking stand for in each measuring jug?

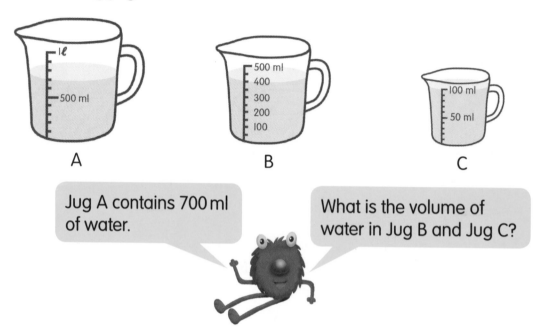

A   B   C

Jug A contains 700 ml of water.

What is the volume of water in Jug B and Jug C?

5 Find the total volume of water in each set of measuring jugs.

a

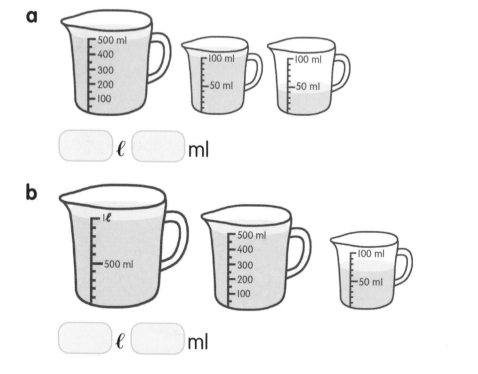

[ ] ℓ [ ] ml

b

[ ] ℓ [ ] ml

c

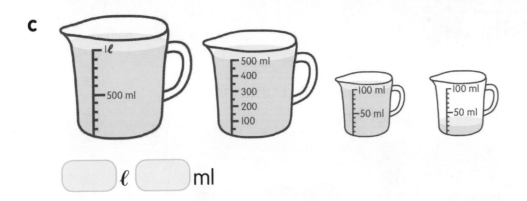

[ ] ℓ [ ] ml

6 Each tank is completely filled with water.
The water in the tank is emptied into some measuring jugs.
Find the capacity of each tank.
Give your answers in litres and millilitres.

a

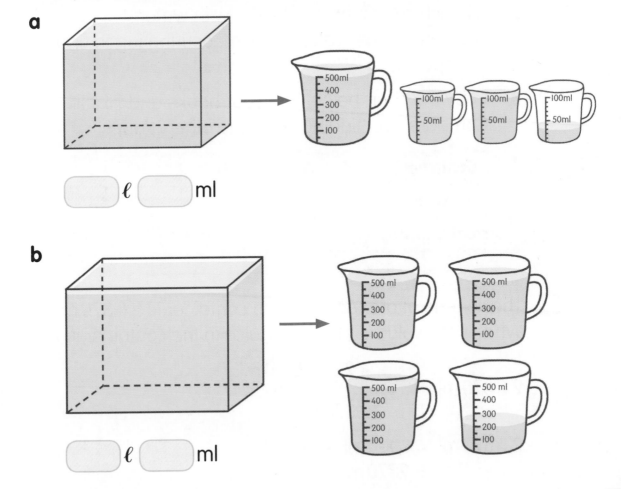

[ ] ℓ [ ] ml

b

[ ] ℓ [ ] ml

Activity

7. You will need four different containers.
   Work in groups of four.

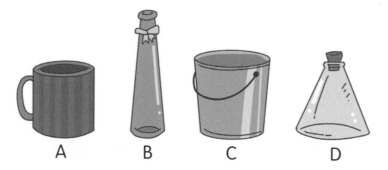

A   B   C   D

1. Estimate the capacity of each container.

2. Fill each container to the brim with water.
   Then empty the water into a measuring jug to find
   its capacity.

3. Copy the chart below into your books and fill it in.
   Compare your findings with the other groups.

Container	A	B	C	D
My Estimate				
Actual Capacity				

8. The volume of orange juice in a container is $2\,\ell\ 370\,\text{ml}$.
   What is the volume of orange juice in the container in millilitres?

$$2\,\ell\ 370\,\text{ml} < \begin{matrix} 2\,\ell = 2000\,\text{ml} \\ 370\,\text{ml} \end{matrix}$$

$$2\,\ell\ 370\,\text{ml} = 2000\,\text{ml} + 370\,\text{ml}$$
$$= 2370\,\text{ml}$$

The volume of orange juice in the container is 2370 ml.

9 The capacity of a barrel is 8725 ml.
What is the capacity of the barrel in litres and millilitres?

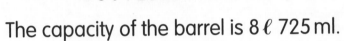

8725 ml $\longleftarrow$ 8000 ml = 8 ℓ

725 ml

8725 ml = 8000 ml + 725 ml
= 8 ℓ 725 ml

The capacity of the barrel is 8 ℓ 725 ml.

10 Complete the following:

7 ℓ 745 ml $\longleftarrow$ ⬭ ℓ = ⬭ ml

⬭ ml

7 ℓ 745 ml = ⬭ ml

11 Complete the following:

4695 ml $\longleftarrow$ ⬭ ml = ⬭ ℓ

⬭ ml

4695 ml = ⬭ ℓ ⬭ ml

12 Write the volume in millilitres.

a 3 ℓ 690 ml   b 5 ℓ 45 ml   c 8 ℓ 8 ml

13 Write the volume in litres and millilitres.

a 4928 ml   b 7090 ml   c 9008 ml

Practice Book 3C, p.39

Put On Your Thinking Caps!

14 **a** The total length of Ribbon A and Ribbon B was 30 cm.
Miya cut 3 cm from Ribbon A.
After that, Ribbon B was twice as long as Ribbon A.
What was the final length of Ribbon A?

A

B

b Omar has 4 bottles of water.
One of the bottles contains 400 ml of water.
Each of the other 3 bottles contains an equal volume
of water.
The total volume of water in the 4 bottles is 760 ml.
What is the volume of water in each of the other 3 bottles?

c Peter has three coins.
One is a fake coin and it is lighter than a real coin.
With the help of the balance below, how can you tell
which is the fake coin?

Say how you get your answer in two different situations:
- when you choose the two real coins first.
- when you choose one real coin and one fake coin.

Unit 12

Solving Word Problems: Length, Mass and Volume

Let's Learn!

One-step word problems

1 Ruby ties a parcel with a piece of string 75 cm long.
She ties another parcel with a piece of string 255 cm long.
What is the total length of the two pieces of string?
Give your answer in metres and centimetres.

$$75 + 255 = 330$$
$$330 \, cm = 3 \, m \, 30 \, cm$$

1 m = 100 cm
3 m = 300 cm
330 cm = 3 m 30 cm

```
      7 5
+   2 5 5
    3 3 0
    1 1
```

The total length of the two pieces of string is 3 m 30 cm.

2 What is the total mass of the two lots of carrots?

◯ ◯ ◯ = ◯

◯ g = ◯ kg ◯ g

The total mass of the carrots
is ◯ kg ◯ g.

Home Maths — Remind your child to give their answers in the correct units.

45

3 The distance between Town A and Town B is 420 km.
The distance between Town B and Town C is 28 km.
What is the difference between the two distances?

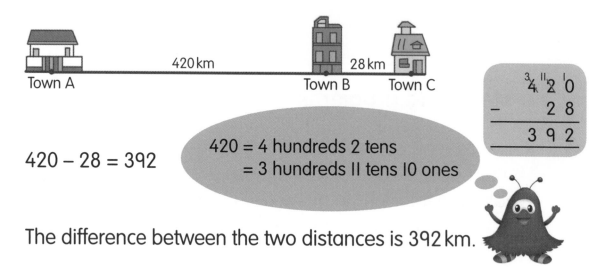

$$420 - 28 = 392$$

420 = 4 hundreds 2 tens
= 3 hundreds 11 tens 10 ones

The difference between the two distances is 392 km.

4 The mass of a box of apples is 38 kg.
The mass of a box of oranges is 24 kg.
How much heavier are the apples than the oranges?

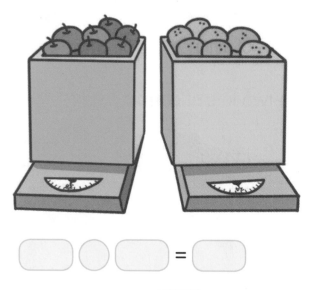

◯ ◯ ◯ = ◯

The apples are ◯ kg heavier than the oranges.

Home Maths Measure the heights of the people in your family. Then find the sums or differences in the heights. Use a weighing scale to find the masses of the people in your family. Then find the sums or differences in the masses.

5 Peter has 4 pieces of wool that each have the same length of 178 cm. What is the total length of wool he has?

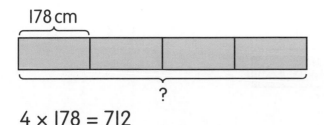

178 cm

?

$$4 \times 178 = 712$$

```
  1 7 8
×     4
-------
  7 1 2
  3 3
```

The total length of wool he has is 712 cm.

6 Hardeep puts some grapes equally into 5 bags.
The mass of each bag of grapes is 125 g.
What is the total mass of the 5 bags of grapes?

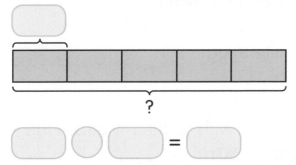

?

( ) ( ) ( ) = ( )

The total mass of the 5 bags of grapes is ( ) g.

7 Mr Robert has 344 ℓ of petrol.
He pours the petrol equally into 8 containers.
How many litres of petrol are there in each container?

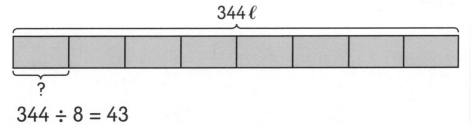

344 ℓ

?

$$344 \div 8 = 43$$

```
      4 3
   -------
 8 ) 3 4 4
     3 2
   -------
       2 4
       2 4
   -------
         0
```

There are 43 ℓ of petrol in each container.

Home Maths

Find out the amount of water each of you drinks at home.
Then write some word problems using this information.

8 Tai cuts a ribbon 135 cm long into 5 pieces.
What is the length of each piece?

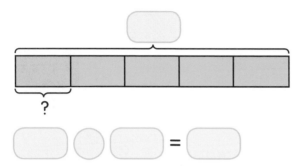

( ) ( ) ( ) = ( )

The length of each piece of ribbon is ( ) cm.

9 Solve these word problems.

a Farha fills up a jug with 728 ml of water.
Her jug contains 95 ml less water than Millie's jug.
How much water is in Millie's jug?

b Peter has 1000 ml of milk in a jug.
He completely fills some cups with all the milk from the jug.
The capacity of each cup is 250 ml.
How many cups does he fill?

c Ruby's aunt buys 108 kg of flour for her shop.
She repacks the flour equally into 9 bags.
How many kilograms of flour are there in each bag?

Practice Book 3C, p.43

Let's Learn!

Two-step word problems

1 Sophia cut a length of string into 7 pieces and had 9 cm left. Each of the 7 pieces of string was 28 cm long.

 a What was the total length of the 7 pieces of string?

 b How much string did Sophia have to begin with? Give your answer in metres and centimetres.

a $28 \times 7 = 196$

28 cm

$$
\begin{array}{r}
2\ 8 \\
\times\quad 7 \\
\hline
1\ 9\ 6 \\
{\scriptstyle 5}
\end{array}
$$

The total length of the 7 pieces of string was 196 cm.

b

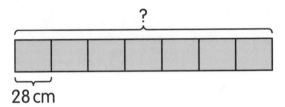

$$
\begin{array}{r}
1\ 9\ 6 \\
+\quad 9 \\
\hline
\boxed{} \\
\hline
\end{array}
$$

$196 + 9 = \boxed{}$

$\boxed{}$ cm = $\boxed{}$ m $\boxed{}$ cm

Sophia had $\boxed{}$ m $\boxed{}$ cm of string to begin with.

2 Dan and Scott competed in a race.
They had to run from Point A to Point B and back again.
The distance between Point A and Point B was 27 km.
When Dan had completed the race, Scott had only run 18 km.
How much further did Scott have to run to complete the race?

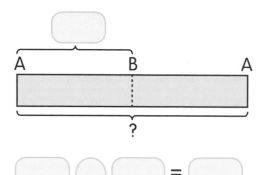

First find the total distance of the race.

The total distance of the race was ⬚ km.

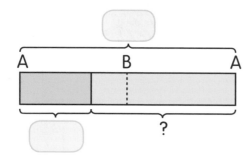

Scott had to run another ⬚ km to complete the race.

3 Ella buys 3 bags of pasta and a big bottle of water.
The mass of each bag of pasta is 500 g.
The 3 bags of pasta are 475 g lighter than the bottle of water.

a What is the mass of the 3 bags of pasta?

b What is the mass of the big bottle of water?

a

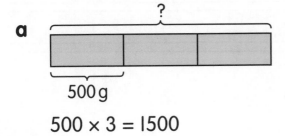

500 × 3 = 1500

The mass of the 3 bags of pasta is
1500 g.

b

The mass of the bottle of water is ⬭ g.

4 Jack had 780 g of tomatoes.
He used 250 g of them to make tomato soup.
Then he packed the remaining tomatoes into 2 bags equally.
What was the mass of each bag of tomatoes?

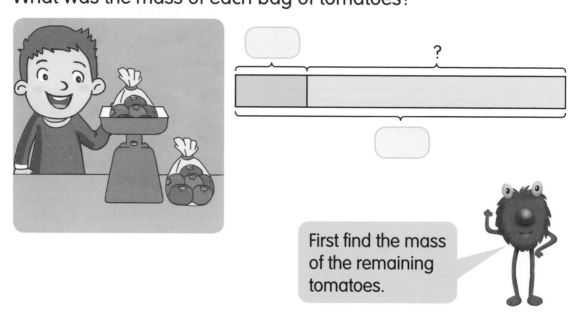

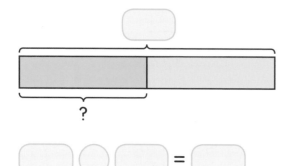

First find the mass of the remaining tomatoes.

⬭ ◯ ⬭ = ⬭

The mass of the remaining tomatoes was ⬭ g.

⬭ ◯ ⬭ = ⬭

The mass of each bag of tomatoes was ⬭ g.

5 A barrel contained some water.
Rhys poured out 27 ℓ of water to fill some buckets to the brim with water.
The capacity of each bucket was 3 ℓ.

a How many buckets were needed to contain the 27 ℓ of water?

b Abby used 5 buckets of water to fill her fish tank.
How many buckets of water were left?

a

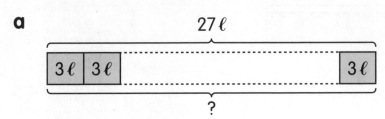

27 ÷ 3 = 9

9 buckets were needed to contain the 27 ℓ of water.

b

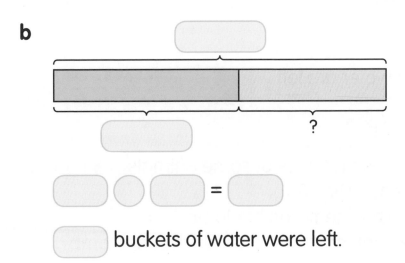

( ) ( ) ( ) = ( )

( ) buckets of water were left.

6 Tai stacks 6 plastic cups into a pyramid.
Each plastic cup contains 310 ml of water.

   a Find the total volume of water in the 6 cups.

   b One cup falls over onto the table.
      How much water is left?

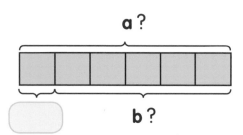

a ◯ ◯ ◯ = ◯

   The total volume of water in the 6 cups is ◯ ml.

b ◯ ◯ ◯ = ◯

   ◯ ml of water are left.

7 Solve these word problems.

   a A vet measures the mass of some animals.
      The sheep's mass is 63 kg.
      She is 3 times as heavy as her lamb.
      What is the total mass of the sheep and her lamb?

   b Ahmed had 225 ml of juice in a jug to start with.
      He then poured 3 glasses of juice into the jug and filled it
      to the brim.
      Each glass contained 175 ml of juice.
      What was the capacity of the jug?

Practice Book 3C, p.47

Activity

8 Work in pairs. Work together to write three two-step word problems. Then solve them.

You can use these words, numbers and units.

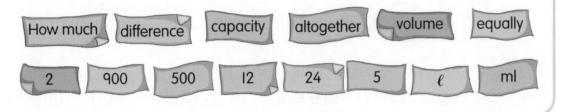

| How much | difference | capacity | altogether | volume | equally |

| 2 | 900 | 500 | 12 | 24 | 5 | ℓ | ml |

Put On Your Thinking Caps!

9 **a** The total length of rope that Millie and Peter have is 284 cm. Peter cuts some of his rope and gives it to Millie. In the end, the length of rope that Millie has is 4 cm shorter than the length of rope that Peter has. What is the length of rope that Millie has left in the end?

b Ruby has a 12 ℓ bucket and a 5 ℓ bucket. How can she get the following amounts of water using these buckets?

2 ℓ   3 ℓ

Practice Book 3C, p.53

Unit 13 Bar Graphs

Let's Learn!

Making bar graphs with scales

1 Four children went to look for butterflies.
Hardeep uses a picture graph to show how many butterflies each child saw.

William		6
Alisha		12
Tom		10
Sophie		8

Each 🦋 stands for 1 butterfly.

Hardeep then uses ☐ to stand for 2 butterflies in the graph below.

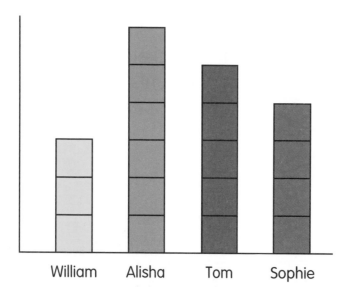

Miss Scott uses another way to show how many butterflies they saw.
The number of butterflies can be read from the graphs below.

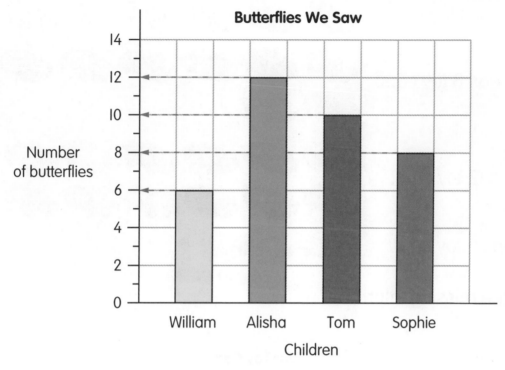

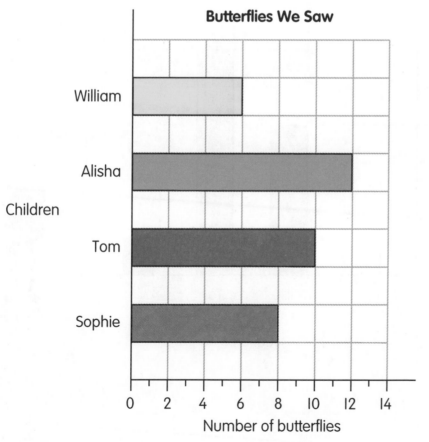

2 The bar graph shows the following information:

Jack has 6 toy cars.

Millie has 8 toy cars.

Tai has 12 toy cars.

Ella has 2 toy cars.

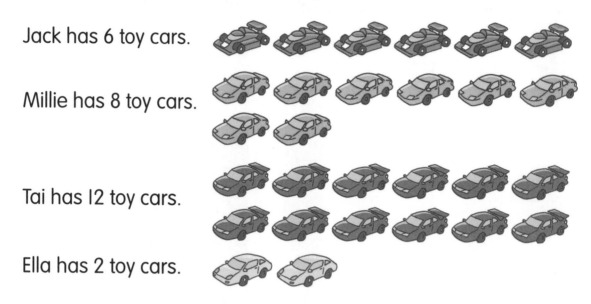

Find the missing information.

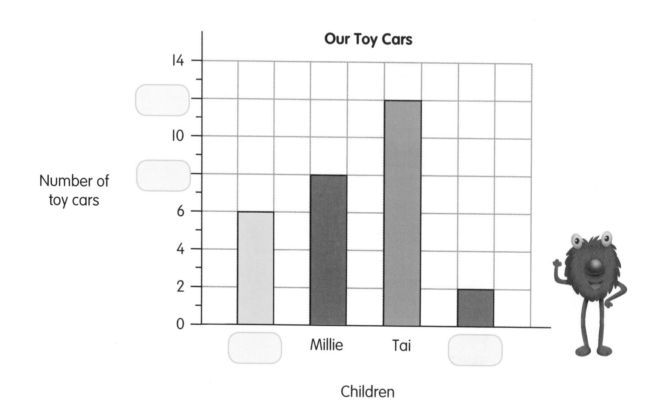

3 The children are folding paper objects.

The number of each type of paper object that they make is shown below.

18 paper aeroplanes

15 paper balls

21 paper boats

12 paper cranes

6 paper frogs

Copy the bar graph.
Show the number of paper objects on the graph.

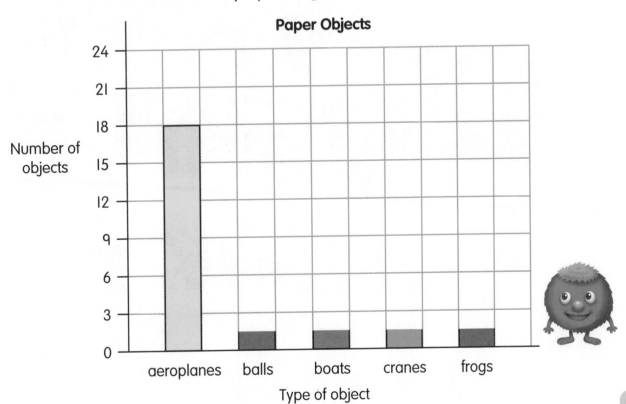

Activity

4 Farha is recording the animals she sees at the park.
Help her count each type of animal she sees.

Activity

Help Farha record her findings. Write the answers in your exercise book.

12				
frogs	dragonflies	spiders	butterflies	ladybirds

Show the findings on a graph like the one below.

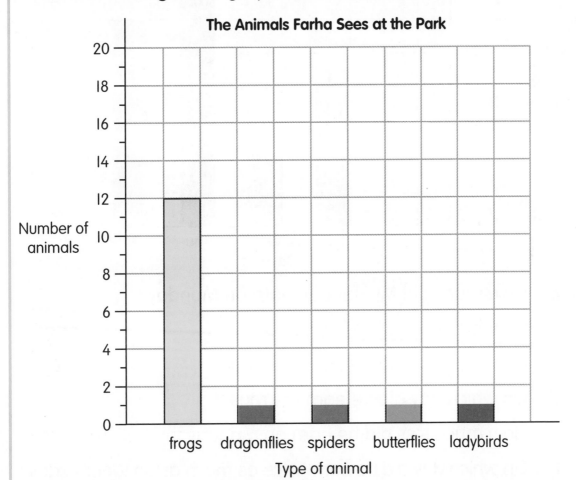

The Animals Farha Sees at the Park

Ask your friends questions based on your bar graph.

Practice Book 3C, p.63

Let's Learn!

Reading and interpreting bar graphs

1 Mr Haddon sold pancakes from Monday to Friday last week. He drew a bar graph to show the amount he earned from selling pancakes for five days.

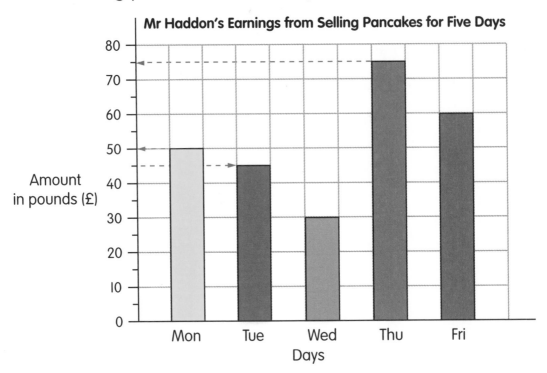

Mr Haddon's Earnings from Selling Pancakes for Five Days

Amount in pounds (£)

Days

a How much did Mr Haddon earn on Monday?

b On which day did he earn £45?

c On which day did he earn the least?

d On which day did he earn the most?

e How much less did he earn on Monday than on Thursday?

f On which day did he earn twice as much as on Wednesday?

Can you give a possible reason why he earned the least on a certain day?

2 Ella's mum owns a stationery shop. Ella draws a bar graph to show the amount of each type of colouring pen and pencil in her mum's shop.

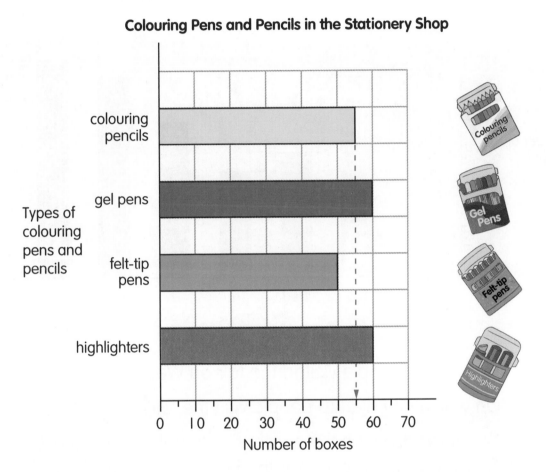

Colouring Pens and Pencils in the Stationery Shop

Find the missing answers.

a How many boxes of colouring pencils are there?

b There are 50 boxes of one type of colouring pens or pencils. Which type is it?

c There are ⬚ more boxes of gel pens than colouring pencils.

d The stationery shop has the same number of boxes of ⬚ as ⬚.

e The stationery shop has 10 fewer boxes of ⬚ than highlighters.

3 The bar graph shows the number of adults and children who visited a fair from Monday to Sunday.

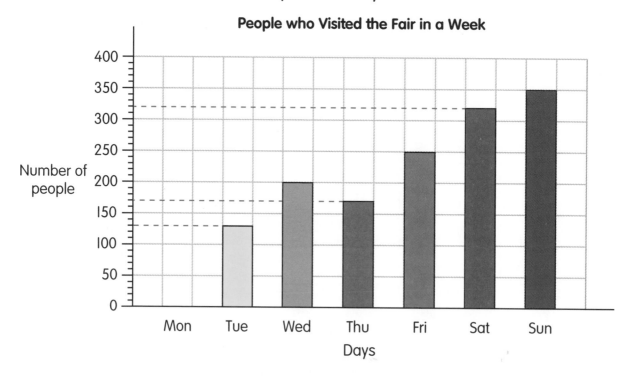

People who Visited the Fair in a Week

a How many people visited the fair on Wednesday?

b On which day did 170 people visit the fair?

c On which day was the number of people the greatest?
Can you give a reason for this?

d On which day were there no visitors at the fair?
Can you give a reason for this?

e On which day were there 150 more people than on Thursday?

f On which day were there 120 fewer people than on Friday?

g On Sunday, 125 adults visited the fair.
How many children visited the fair on that day?

4 The bar graph shows the amount of money spent in a day by Chantal and her friends.

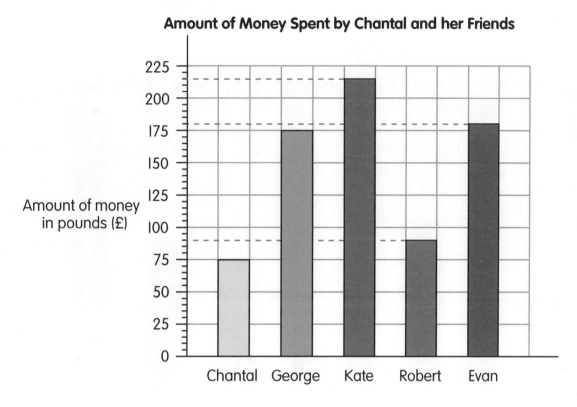

Amount of Money Spent by Chantal and her Friends

Amount of money in pounds (£)

Chantal George Kate Robert Evan

a How much did Kate spend?

b Who spent £90?

c Who spent the most money?
Can you give a reason for this?

d Who spent the least money?
How much did she spend?

e How much more did Kate spend than Chantal?

f Who spent twice as much money as Robert?

g If Evan wants to spend twice as much money as George, how much more money should he spend?

Practice Book 3C, p.71

Let's Explore!

5 The bar graph shows the number of books borrowed from the library over five days.

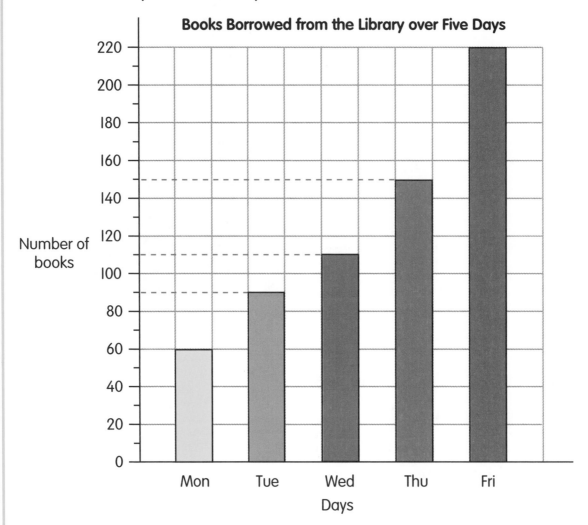

Read the graph.
Write three questions about it.
You can use the words below to help you.

| how many books | more than | fewer than | twice as |
| many as | the least | the most | on which day |

Put On Your Thinking Caps!

6 Read the following information.

The number of children wearing shoes with buckles is 18.
There are 7 more children wearing shoes with laces than
slip-on shoes.
There are 10 fewer children wearing slip-on shoes than shoes
with buckles.

Look at bar graphs A, B and C.
Which bar graph shows **all** the information in the
green box **correctly**?

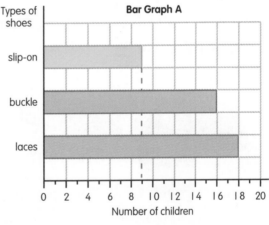

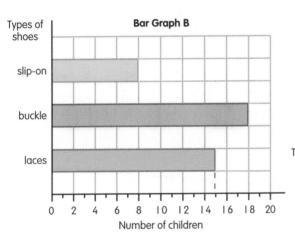

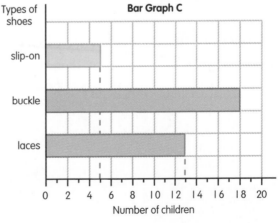

Practice Book 3C, p.75

Let's Learn!

Numerator and denominator

 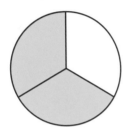

$\frac{2}{3}$ ← numerator
← denominator

In the fraction $\frac{2}{3}$, 2 is the **numerator**, and 3 is the **denominator**.

2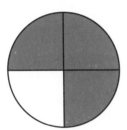

_____ of the circle is shaded.

The numerator of the fraction is _____.

The denominator of the fraction is _____.

3 The numerator of a fraction is twice as large as 4.
The denominator of the fraction is 7 more than the numerator.
What is the fraction? _____

Practice Book 3C, p.77

Let's Learn!

Understanding equivalent fractions

1 Look at these fraction strips.

1

One whole

$\frac{1}{2}$	$\frac{1}{2}$

1 out of 2 equal parts $= \frac{1}{2}$

$\frac{1}{4}$	$\frac{1}{4}$	$\frac{1}{4}$	$\frac{1}{4}$

2 out of 4 equal parts $= \frac{2}{4}$

$\frac{1}{8}$	$\frac{1}{8}$	$\frac{1}{8}$	$\frac{1}{8}$	$\frac{1}{8}$	$\frac{1}{8}$	$\frac{1}{8}$	$\frac{1}{8}$

4 out of 8 equal parts $= \frac{4}{8}$

The fractions $\frac{1}{2}$, $\frac{2}{4}$ and $\frac{4}{8}$ have different numerators and denominators.

$\frac{1}{2}$ is equal to $\frac{2}{4}$.

$\frac{1}{2}$ is also equal to $\frac{4}{8}$.

$\frac{1}{2}$, $\frac{2}{4}$ and $\frac{4}{8}$ are **equivalent fractions**.

2 Name some equivalent fractions of $\frac{2}{3}$.

a

$\frac{2}{3}$ of the bar is shaded.

b

$$\frac{2}{3} = \frac{\bigcirc}{6}$$

c

$$\frac{2}{3} = \frac{\bigcirc}{9}$$

69

Activity

3 You will need three strips of paper that are the same size.

1 Fold the first strip into three equal parts. Then unfold the strip and draw lines along the folds to divide it into three equal parts.

2 Shade one part of the first strip.
You get the shaded fraction $\frac{1}{3}$.

3 Refold the first strip.
Then fold it in half again.
You will find that an equivalent fraction of the shaded fraction $\frac{1}{3}$ is $\frac{2}{6}$.

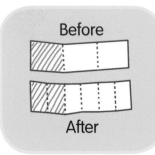

Before

After

4 Make the following shaded fractions with the remaining strips:
$\frac{1}{4}$ and $\frac{3}{4}$.
Then fold these strips again to find their equivalent fractions.

Home Maths   Ask your child to help you cut up some food (for example, an orange, a cake or a pizza) to show equivalent fractions.

4 What are the missing numerators and denominators of these equivalent fractions?

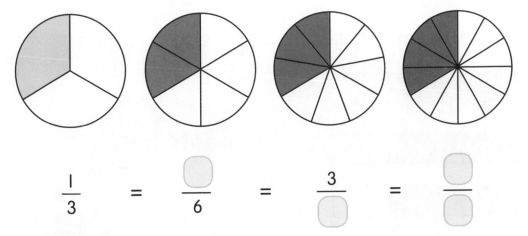

$$\frac{1}{3} \quad = \quad \frac{\boxed{}}{6} \quad = \quad \frac{3}{\boxed{}} \quad = \quad \frac{\boxed{}}{\boxed{}}$$

Activity

5

1 Draw a table with I row and 4 equal columns.
Shade the first column.

2 Then draw a table with I row and 8 equal columns.
Shade the first 2 columns.

3 Finally draw a table with I row and 12 equal columns.
Shade the first 3 columns.

What do you notice about the shaded parts?
What fraction of each table is shaded?

All three tables should be the same width and height.

Practice Book 3C, p.79

Let's Learn!

More equivalent fractions: short cut

 $\frac{2}{3}$

$\frac{4}{6}$

$\frac{6}{9}$

$\frac{8}{12}$

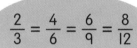 $\frac{2}{3} = \frac{4}{6} = \frac{6}{9} = \frac{8}{12}$

There is a short cut!
To find an equivalent fraction,
multiply the numerator and the
denominator by the same number.

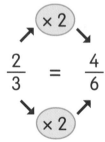

$\times 2$

$\frac{2}{3} = \frac{4}{6}$

$\times 2$

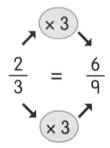

$\times 3$

$\frac{2}{3} = \frac{6}{9}$

$\times 3$

To get $\frac{8}{12}$, we **multiply**
the numerator and
denominator of $\frac{2}{3}$ by ⬚.

2 Use multiplication to find:

a the first three equivalent fractions of $\frac{1}{7}$.

$$\frac{1}{7} = \frac{\boxed{}}{\boxed{}} \quad (\times 2)$$

$$\frac{1}{7} = \frac{\boxed{}}{\boxed{}} \quad (\times 3)$$

$$\frac{1}{7} = \frac{\boxed{}}{\boxed{}} \quad (\times 4)$$

$$\frac{1}{7} = \frac{\boxed{}}{\boxed{}} = \frac{\boxed{}}{\boxed{}} = \frac{\boxed{}}{\boxed{}}$$

b the first eight equivalent fractions of $\frac{3}{5}$.

$$\frac{3}{5} = \frac{\boxed{}}{\boxed{}} = \frac{\boxed{}}{\boxed{}} = \frac{\boxed{}}{\boxed{}} = \frac{\boxed{}}{\boxed{}} = \frac{\boxed{}}{\boxed{}} = \frac{\boxed{}}{\boxed{}} = \frac{\boxed{}}{\boxed{}} = \frac{\boxed{}}{\boxed{}}$$

3 Complete these equivalent fractions:

a $\dfrac{3}{4} = \dfrac{\boxed{}}{8} = \dfrac{9}{\boxed{}}$

b $\dfrac{2}{5} = \dfrac{4}{\boxed{}} = \dfrac{\boxed{}}{15}$

c $\dfrac{1}{3} = \dfrac{2}{\boxed{}} = \dfrac{\boxed{}}{9}$

Practice Book 3C, p.81

4 Here is another way of finding equivalent fractions. **Divide** the numerator and the denominator by the same number.

$$\frac{6}{12} = \frac{3}{6}$$ (÷2)

$$\frac{6}{12} = \frac{2}{4}$$ (÷3)

5 Is $\frac{2}{4}$ the simplest equivalent fraction of $\frac{6}{12}$?

$$\frac{2}{4} = \frac{1}{2}$$ (÷2)

No, you can divide the numerator and denominator of $\frac{2}{4}$ by the same number.

$\frac{1}{2}$ is the **simplest form** of $\frac{2}{4}$.

The simplest equivalent fraction of $\frac{6}{12}$ is $\frac{1}{2}$.

You use division when you want to find a fraction in its simplest form.

6 Complete the following equivalent fractions of $\frac{4}{12}$.

$$\frac{4}{12} = \frac{\boxed{}}{6}$$

$$\frac{4}{12} = \frac{1}{\boxed{}}$$

The simplest equivalent fraction of $\frac{4}{12}$ is $\frac{\boxed{}}{\boxed{}}$.

Practice Book 3C, p.83

Let's Learn!

Comparing fractions

1 Ruby had $\frac{1}{2}$ of a pie.

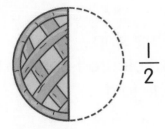

$\frac{1}{2}$

Peter had $\frac{3}{4}$ of an identical pie.

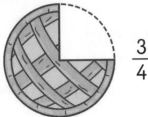

$\frac{3}{4}$

Omar had $\frac{1}{4}$ of another identical pie.

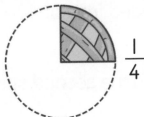

$\frac{1}{4}$

Peter had a bigger portion than Ruby.

$\frac{3}{4}$ is greater than $\frac{1}{2}$.

Omar had a smaller portion than Ruby.

$\frac{1}{4}$ is smaller than $\frac{1}{2}$.

Activity

2 You will need two strips of paper that are the same size.

1 Fold the first strip in half.

2 Unfold the strip.
Using a coloured pencil, draw a line along the fold.

3 Refold the strip.
Then fold it in half twice.

4 Unfold the strip.
Using a different coloured pencil, draw lines along the new folds.

5 Shade to show a fraction greater than $\frac{1}{2}$.

The shaded fraction is $\dfrac{\bigcirc}{\bigcirc}$.

6 Now fold the second strip in half and repeat steps 2 to 4.

7 Shade a fraction which is smaller than $\frac{1}{2}$.

The shaded fraction is $\dfrac{\bigcirc}{\bigcirc}$.

3 Which is greater, $\frac{5}{6}$ or $\frac{1}{2}$?

$\frac{5}{6}$ 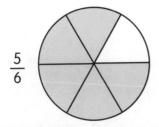 $\frac{1}{2}$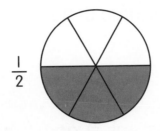

Which is smaller, $\frac{7}{8}$ or $\frac{1}{2}$?

$\frac{7}{8}$ 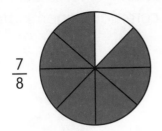 $\frac{1}{2}$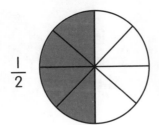

4 Pie A and Pie B are the same size.

Omar's mum cut $\frac{3}{4}$ of Pie A for Omar.

She cut $\frac{7}{8}$ of Pie B for Ruby.

Who got a bigger portion?
Who got a smaller portion?

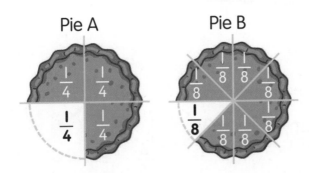

First find an equivalent fraction of $\frac{3}{4}$

that has the same denominator as $\frac{7}{8}$.

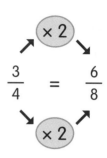

Now the fractions $\frac{6}{8}$ and $\frac{7}{8}$ have a **common denominator**.

Compare the fractions.

> It's easy to compare fractions when they have a common denominator.

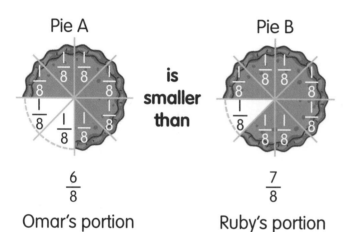

Pie A

is smaller than

Pie B

$\frac{6}{8}$

Omar's portion

$\frac{7}{8}$

Ruby's portion

The greater fraction is the one with the greater numerator.
The smaller fraction is the one with the smaller numerator.

Ruby got a bigger portion and Omar got a smaller portion.

5 Which is the greater fraction, $\frac{1}{2}$ or $\frac{4}{10}$?

The greater fraction is ⬚.

6 Which is the smaller fraction, $\frac{3}{12}$ or $\frac{2}{4}$?

The smaller fraction is ⬚.

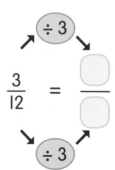

$$\frac{3}{12} = \frac{\Box}{\Box}$$

7 Which fraction is greater, $\dfrac{3}{5}$ or $\dfrac{3}{6}$?

As the fractions have the **same numerator**, compare their denominators!

 $\dfrac{3}{5}$

is greater than

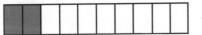 $\dfrac{3}{6}$

The greater fraction is the one with the smaller denominator.

8 Which fraction is smaller, $\dfrac{2}{10}$ or $\dfrac{2}{7}$?

It's easy to compare fractions when they have a **common numerator**.

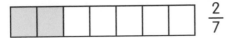 $\dfrac{2}{10}$

is smaller than

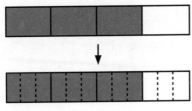 $\dfrac{2}{7}$

The smaller fraction is the one with the greater denominator.

9 Which fraction is greater, $\dfrac{3}{4}$ or $\dfrac{1}{6}$?

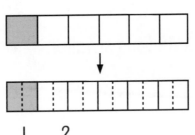

$\dfrac{3}{4} = \dfrac{6}{8} = \dfrac{9}{12}$ $\dfrac{1}{6} = \dfrac{2}{12}$

$\dfrac{9}{12}$ is greater than $\dfrac{2}{12}$.

$$\overset{\times 3}{\dfrac{3}{4} = \dfrac{9}{12}}\underset{\times 3}{} \qquad \overset{\times 2}{\dfrac{1}{6} = \dfrac{2}{12}}\underset{\times 2}{}$$

$\dfrac{3}{4}$ is greater than $\dfrac{1}{6}$.

Activity

10 Which fraction is greater?
Use fraction shapes to help you!

a $\frac{4}{9}$ or $\frac{2}{3}$ ⬜ **b** $\frac{2}{4}$ or $\frac{2}{12}$ ⬜

c $\frac{3}{8}$ or $\frac{2}{4}$ ⬜ **d** $\frac{2}{3}$ or $\frac{3}{5}$ ⬜

11 Answer these questions.

a Which is smaller, $\frac{2}{3}$ or $\frac{7}{9}$?

$$\frac{2}{3} = \frac{\bigcirc}{9}$$

b Which is greater, $\frac{5}{6}$ or $\frac{3}{4}$?

$$\frac{5}{6} = \frac{\bigcirc}{12} \qquad \frac{3}{4} = \frac{\bigcirc}{12}$$

c Which is smaller, $\frac{5}{6}$ or $\frac{3}{8}$?

d Which is greater, $\frac{6}{7}$ or $\frac{1}{3}$?

Compare the fractions to see which is greater or smaller than $\frac{1}{2}$.

e Write any three fractions, two of which are smaller than $\frac{3}{4}$.

f Write any three fractions, two of which are greater than $\frac{1}{2}$.

12 Arrange the fractions in order, beginning with the smallest.

$$\frac{1}{2}, \frac{5}{6}, \frac{1}{12}$$

Method 1

Let's compare $\frac{5}{6}$ and $\frac{1}{12}$ with $\frac{1}{2}$.

$\frac{5}{6}$ 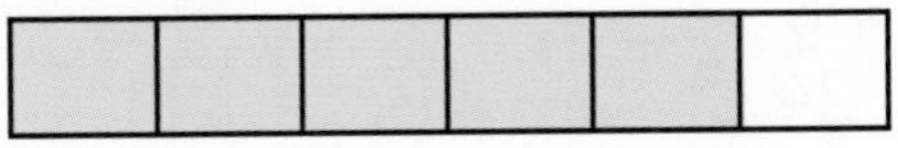 $\frac{1}{12}$

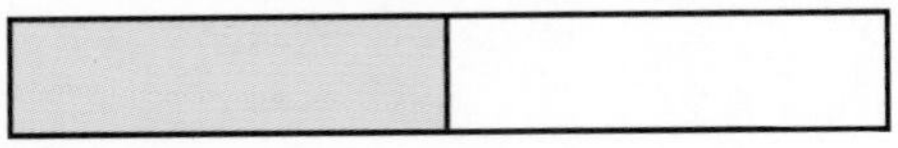

$\frac{1}{2}$ $\frac{1}{2}$

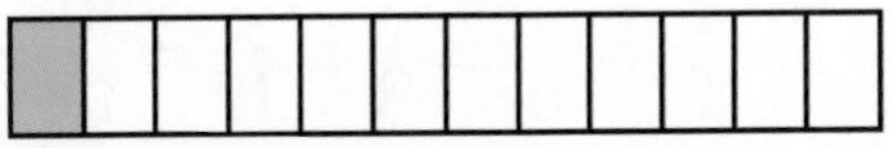

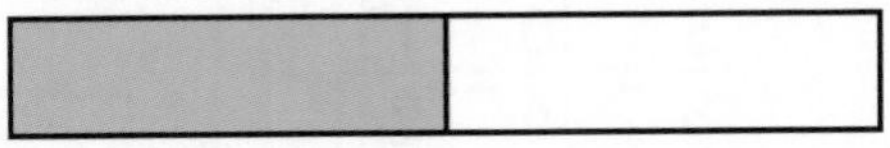

$\frac{5}{6}$ is greater than $\frac{1}{2}$. $\frac{1}{12}$ is smaller than $\frac{1}{2}$.

$$\frac{1}{12}, \frac{1}{2}, \frac{5}{6}$$
↑
smallest

Method 2

Express all the fractions with the same denominator 12.

$$\frac{1}{2} = \frac{6}{12} \qquad\qquad \frac{5}{6} = \frac{10}{12}$$

$\frac{1}{12}$ is smaller than $\frac{1}{2}$. $\frac{5}{6}$ is greater than $\frac{1}{2}$.

$$\frac{1}{12}, \frac{1}{2}, \frac{5}{6}$$
↑
smallest

13 Arrange the fractions in order, beginning with:

a the greatest: $\frac{7}{8}, \frac{1}{4}, \frac{1}{2}$ **b** the smallest: $\frac{1}{2}, \frac{9}{10}, \frac{2}{5}$

14 Arrange the fractions in order, beginning with the greatest.

$$\frac{2}{3}, \frac{5}{8}, \frac{3}{4}$$

Express all the fractions with the same denominator.
First make a list of equivalent fractions.

$$\frac{2}{3} = \frac{4}{6} = \frac{6}{9} = \frac{8}{12} = \frac{10}{15} = \frac{12}{18} = \frac{14}{21} = \frac{16}{24}$$

$$\frac{5}{8} = \frac{10}{16} = \frac{15}{24}$$

$$\frac{3}{4} = \frac{6}{8} = \frac{9}{12} = \frac{12}{16} = \frac{15}{20} = \frac{18}{24}$$

$\frac{16}{24}$ is greater than $\frac{15}{24}$.

Therefore $\frac{2}{3}$ is greater than $\frac{5}{8}$.

$\frac{18}{24}$ is greater than $\frac{16}{24}$.

Therefore $\frac{3}{4}$ is greater than $\frac{2}{3}$.

$$\frac{3}{4}, \frac{2}{3}, \frac{5}{8}$$
↑
greatest

15 Arrange the fractions in order, beginning with:

a the greatest: $\frac{1}{2}, \frac{5}{8}, \frac{1}{3}$

b the smallest: $\frac{7}{12}, \frac{4}{9}, \frac{1}{6}$

Practice Book 3C, p.85

Let's Explore!

16 Hardeep, Miya and Millie each have a fraction strip.
Hardeep's fraction is greater than Miya's and Millie's.
Miya's fraction is smaller than Millie's.

Hardeep

Miya

Millie

Look at Hardeep's fraction strip. Trace and cut out Miya's and
Millie's strips onto a piece of paper. Then divide each strip into
a different number of equal parts by folding.

What could Miya's and Millie's fractions be?
Shade the parts of each strip to show possible answers.
Then write down and check your answers.

Can you think of any other possible answers?

Maths Journal

17 Peter folded Miya's strip in half and Millie's strip into six equal
parts. He wrote the first step to his answers.

First I fold and shade Miya's fraction strip.

I need to shade a fraction smaller than $\frac{7}{8}$.

I check my answer: $\frac{1}{2} = \frac{4}{8}$.

$\frac{1}{2}$ is smaller than $\frac{7}{8}$.

Now write down all the steps to your answers.

Let's Learn!

Adding fractions

1 Peter eats $\frac{1}{3}$ of a pizza.

Farha eats $\frac{1}{6}$ of the same pizza.

What fraction of the pizza do they eat altogether?

First find an equivalent fraction of $\frac{1}{3}$ that has the same denominator as $\frac{1}{6}$.

$$\frac{1}{3} \overset{\times 2}{=} \frac{2}{6} \underset{\times 2}{}$$

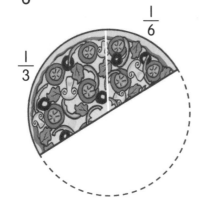 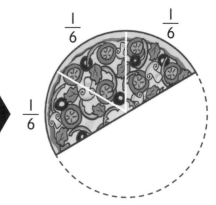

Then add.

$$\frac{1}{3} + \frac{1}{6} = \frac{2}{6} + \frac{1}{6}$$

$$= \frac{3}{6}$$

$$= \frac{1}{2}$$

Always remember to write your answer in its simplest form.

They eat $\frac{1}{2}$ of the pizza altogether.

To add fractions, first change them to fractions with the same denominator.

2 Add $\frac{1}{4}$ and $\frac{3}{8}$.

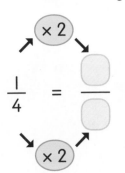

$$\frac{1}{4} = \frac{\boxed{}}{\boxed{}}$$

What fraction is equal to $\frac{1}{4}$ and has the same denominator as $\frac{3}{8}$?

$$\frac{1}{4} + \frac{3}{8} = \frac{\boxed{}}{\boxed{}} + \frac{3}{8}$$

$$= \frac{\boxed{}}{\boxed{}}$$

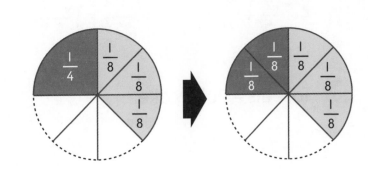

3 Find the equivalent fraction.
Complete the model.
Then add the fractions.

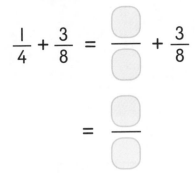

$$\frac{1}{3} = \frac{\boxed{}}{\boxed{}}$$

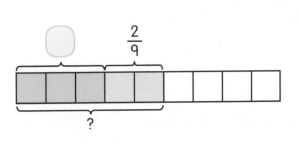

$$\frac{1}{3} + \frac{2}{9} = \frac{\boxed{}}{\boxed{}} + \frac{\boxed{}}{\boxed{}}$$

$$= \frac{\boxed{}}{\boxed{}}$$

4 Find the sum.

a $\dfrac{1}{2} + \dfrac{1}{4} = \dfrac{\boxed{}}{\boxed{}} + \dfrac{1}{4} = \dfrac{\boxed{}}{\boxed{}}$

b $\dfrac{1}{3} + \dfrac{1}{9} = \dfrac{\boxed{}}{\boxed{}} + \dfrac{\boxed{}}{\boxed{}} = \dfrac{\boxed{}}{\boxed{}}$

c $\dfrac{2}{5} + \dfrac{3}{10} = \dfrac{\boxed{}}{\boxed{}} + \dfrac{\boxed{}}{\boxed{}} = \dfrac{\boxed{}}{\boxed{}}$

5 Tai eats $\dfrac{1}{3}$ of a cake.

Miya eats $\dfrac{1}{9}$ of the same cake.

Peter eats $\dfrac{3}{9}$ of the same cake.

What fraction of the cake do they eat altogether?

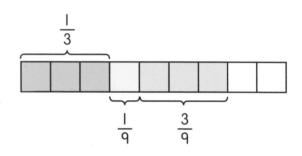

$\dfrac{1}{3} + \dfrac{1}{9} + \dfrac{3}{9} = \dfrac{3}{9} + \dfrac{1}{9} + \dfrac{3}{9}$

$\qquad\qquad = \dfrac{7}{9}$

$\dfrac{1}{3} = \dfrac{3}{9}$

Tai, Miya and Peter eat $\dfrac{7}{9}$ of the cake.

6 Add.

a $\dfrac{1}{5} + \dfrac{2}{10} + \dfrac{3}{10}$ 　　　 b $\dfrac{3}{8} + \dfrac{1}{8} + \dfrac{1}{4}$

c $\dfrac{5}{12} + \dfrac{1}{3} + \dfrac{1}{12}$ 　　　 d $\dfrac{2}{10} + \dfrac{3}{10} + \dfrac{1}{2}$

Practice Book 3C, p.89

Let's Learn!

Subtracting fractions

 I ate $\frac{1}{2}$ of a pizza.

I ate $\frac{3}{8}$ of the same pizza.

 $\frac{1}{2}$

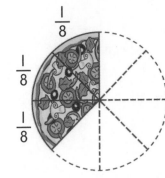

$\frac{1}{8}$

$\frac{1}{8}$

$\frac{1}{8}$

Jack

Millie

Who ate more? How much more?

First find an equivalent fraction of $\frac{1}{2}$ that has the same denominator as $\frac{3}{8}$.

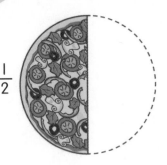

$$\times 4$$

$$\frac{1}{2} = \frac{4}{8}$$

$$\times 4$$

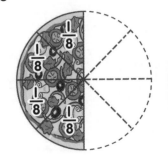

Then subtract.

$$\frac{1}{2} - \frac{3}{8} = \frac{4}{8} - \frac{3}{8}$$

$$= \frac{1}{8}$$

Jack ate $\frac{1}{8}$ more of the pizza than Millie.

To subtract fractions, first change them to fractions with the same denominator.

2 Subtract $\frac{2}{5}$ from $\frac{7}{10}$.

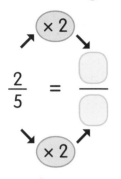

$\frac{2}{5} = \dfrac{\bigcirc}{\bigcirc}$

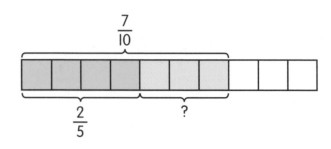

$$\frac{7}{10} - \frac{2}{5} = \frac{\bigcirc}{\bigcirc} - \frac{\bigcirc}{\bigcirc}$$

$$= \frac{\bigcirc}{\bigcirc}$$

3 Find the equivalent fraction.
Complete the model. Then subtract the fractions.

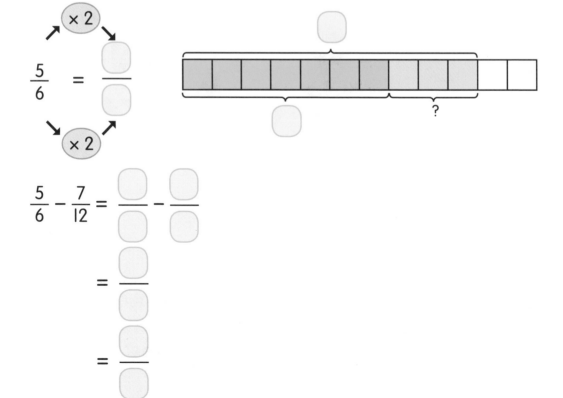

$\frac{5}{6} = \dfrac{\bigcirc}{\bigcirc}$

$$\frac{5}{6} - \frac{7}{12} = \frac{\bigcirc}{\bigcirc} - \frac{\bigcirc}{\bigcirc}$$

$$= \frac{\bigcirc}{\bigcirc}$$

$$= \frac{\bigcirc}{\bigcirc}$$

4 Find the difference.

a $1 - \dfrac{3}{4} = \dfrac{\Box}{\Box} - \dfrac{\Box}{\Box} = \dfrac{\Box}{\Box}$

b $\dfrac{1}{2} - \dfrac{1}{4} = \dfrac{\Box}{\Box} - \dfrac{1}{4} = \dfrac{\Box}{\Box}$

c $\dfrac{2}{3} - \dfrac{5}{9} = \dfrac{\Box}{\Box} - \dfrac{\Box}{\Box} = \dfrac{\Box}{\Box}$

5 Ella ate $\dfrac{2}{5}$ of a pie.

Hardeep ate $\dfrac{3}{10}$ of the same pie.

What fraction of the pie was left?

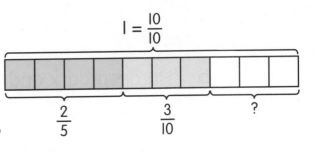

$1 = \dfrac{10}{10}$

$\dfrac{2}{5}$ $\dfrac{3}{10}$?

$1 - \dfrac{2}{5} - \dfrac{3}{10} = \dfrac{10}{10} - \dfrac{4}{10} - \dfrac{3}{10}$

$\qquad\qquad\quad = \dfrac{3}{10}$

$\dfrac{3}{10}$ of the pie was left.

$\dfrac{2}{5} = \dfrac{4}{10}$

6 Subtract.

a $1 - \dfrac{2}{7} - \dfrac{3}{7}$

b $1 - \dfrac{2}{11} - \dfrac{5}{11}$

c $1 - \dfrac{3}{4} - \dfrac{1}{12}$

d $1 - \dfrac{5}{12} - \dfrac{1}{3}$

Practice Book 3C, p.91

Put On Your Thinking Caps!

7 **a** The diagram below shows $\frac{3}{4}$ of a fraction strip shaded. How many of the shaded parts should be rubbed out so that the remaining shaded parts are $\frac{3}{8}$ of the strip?

Try drawing the model in another way.

b Hardeep, Jack and Ella cut a cake into 9 equal pieces.

Hardeep ate $\frac{2}{9}$ of the cake.

Jack ate a greater portion of the cake than Ella.

They finished the whole cake.

What are the possible fractions to show how much cake Jack ate?

What is the greatest fraction of the cake Ella could have had?

Try drawing a model first.

Practice Book 3C, p.93   Practice Book 3C, p.94

15 Time

Let's Learn!

Telling the time

1

I minute

Each small marking stands for I minute.

The minute hand shows 5 minutes past the hour.

2 The children are in the school hall at 9:20 a.m. for the morning assembly.

It is 20 minutes after 9 o'clock.

We say the time is **nine twenty**.

We can also say the time is **20 minutes past 9**.

3 At 5:40 p.m., a group of parents meet in the school.

It's 20 minutes before 6 o'clock.

60 − 40 = 20

The time is **five forty**.

We can also say the time is **20 minutes to 6**.

4 Find the missing numbers.

a

The time is six fifteen. It is ☐ minutes after 6.

6:15 is ☐ minutes past 6.

b

The time is five forty-five. It is ☐ minutes before 6.

5:45 is ☐ minutes to 6.

5 Use **past** or **to**.

a

b

8:07 is 7 minutes ⬭ 8.

2:37 is 23 minutes ⬭ 3.

6 You will need two clock faces.
Position the minute hand to show:

a 25 minutes past 11.

b 18 minutes to 7.

7 What are the missing numbers?

a 9:10 is ⬭ minutes past 9.

b 2:09 is 9 minutes past ⬭.

c 5:48 is ⬭ minutes to 6.

d 7:45 is 15 minutes to ⬭.

 Home Maths Encourage your child to tell the time at home. Use 'past' until the minute hand moves past the half hour.
Use 'to' when the minute hand has moved past the half hour.
For example, 9:20 is 20 minutes past 9 and 8:40 is 20 minutes to 9.

Game

8 **Show and tell the time!**

Players: 2
You will need:
- a clock with movable minute and hour hands

1 Player 1 shows a time by moving the hour hand and the minute hand.

2 Player 2 tells the time in two different ways.

- two fifty
- 10 minutes to 3

3 Player 1 checks the answer. Player 2 gets 1 point for a correct answer.

4 Player 2 shows the time and Player 1 tells the time.

- five seventeen
- 17 minutes past 5

5 Take turns to show and tell the time. Play five rounds.

The player with the most points wins!

Practice Book 3D, p.7

Let's Learn!

Conversion of hours and minutes

1 Tai cycles for 2 hours.
How many minutes are there in 2 hours?

1 h = 60 mins
2 h = 60 mins + 60 mins
    = 120 mins

We can also do it this way:

2 h = 2 × 60 mins
    = 120 mins

There are 120 minutes in 2 hours.

1 h = 60 mins

2 × 6 = 12
2 × 60 = 120
Can you see
the pattern?

2 Tai takes 3 hours to do his homework.
How many minutes are there in 3 hours?

3 h = ◯ mins + ◯ mins + ◯ mins

    = ◯ mins

We can also do it this way:

3 h = ◯ × 60 mins

    = ◯ mins

There are ◯ minutes in 3 hours.

3 × 6 = ◯

3 × 60 = ◯

3 Omar plays badminton for 1h 10 mins.
How many minutes are there in 1h 10 mins?

1h 10 mins = 60 mins + 10 mins
= 70 mins

1h 10 mins $<$ 1h = 60 mins / 10 mins

There are 70 minutes in 1h 10 mins.

4 Miya watches a film for 2h 30 mins.
How many minutes are there in 2h 30 mins?

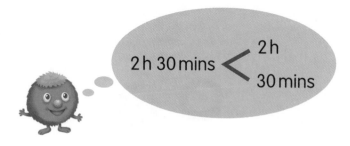

2h 30 mins $<$ 2h / 30 mins

2h 30 mins = ⬚ mins + ⬚ mins + ⬚ mins

= ⬚ mins

There are ⬚ minutes in 2h 30 mins.

5 Write the times in minutes.

a 2h 45 mins

= ⬚ mins + ⬚ mins

= ⬚ mins

b 4h 28 mins

= ⬚ mins + ⬚ mins

= ⬚ mins

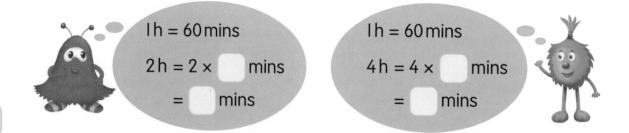

1h = 60 mins

2h = 2 × ⬚ mins

= ⬚ mins

1h = 60 mins

4h = 4 × ⬚ mins

= ⬚ mins

6 Ella takes 135 minutes to wash her dad's car. How many hours and minutes are there in 135 minutes?

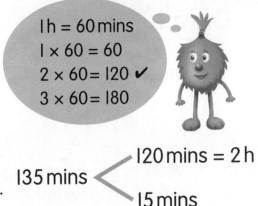

135 mins = 120 mins + 15 mins

       = 2 h 15 mins

There are 2 h 15 mins in 135 minutes.

135 mins ⟨ 120 mins = 2 h

                 15 mins

7 Peter plays the piano for 82 minutes. How many hours and minutes are there in 82 minutes?

82 mins = ⬚ mins + ⬚ mins

      = ⬚ h ⬚ mins

There are ⬚ h ⬚ mins in 82 minutes.

8 Write the times in hours and minutes.

a 90 mins = ⬚ mins + ⬚ mins

         = ⬚ h ⬚ mins

b 130 mins

c 145 mins

d 192 mins

Practice Book 3D, p.9

Game

9 Time bingo!

How to play:

Players: 2 groups of 2 children
You will need:
- time cards
- bingo card

1 Work in groups. Group I draws a card from the stack of time cards.

These are examples of the two types of time cards:

I h 25 mins = ⬚ mins

75 mins = ⬚ h ⬚ mins

2 For a time card that shows time in hours and minutes, change the time to minutes. For example,
$$I h\ 25\ mins = 60\ mins + 25\ mins$$
$$= 85\ mins$$

For a time card that shows time in minutes, change the time to hours and minutes. For example,
$$75\ mins = 60\ mins + 15\ mins$$
$$= I h\ 15\ mins$$

3 The groups take turns to mark their answers on the bingo card. Group I marks their answers with a cross, while Group 2 marks their answers with a circle.

100 mins	60 mins	240 mins
I h 15 mins	2 h 5 mins	45 mins
130 mins	63 mins	3 h

The first group to mark three correct answers in a straight line (↕ , ↔ , ↘) on the bingo card wins.

Let's Learn!

Addition

1 Mr Smith worked 2 h 15 mins in the morning.
He worked 5 h 10 mins in the afternoon.
How long did he work altogether?

2 h 15 mins + 5 h 10 mins = ?

First add the hours.

2 h $\boxed{+ 5 h}$ 7 h

Then add the minutes.

15 mins $\boxed{+ 10 mins}$ 25 mins

2 h 15 mins + 5 h 10 mins = 7 h 25 mins

Mr Smith worked 7 h 25 mins altogether.

2 3 h 20 mins + 4 h 15 mins = ?

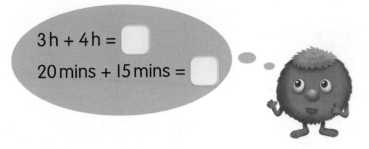

3 h + 4 h = ☐

20 mins + 15 mins = ☐

3 h 20 mins + 4 h 15 mins = ☐ h ☐ mins

3 Emily was taking a flight from London to Paris.
She waited 40 minutes to check in her luggage.
Then she waited 1 h 55 mins before boarding the aeroplane.
How long did she wait altogether?

40 mins + 1 h 55 mins = ?

First add the minutes.
40 mins + 55 mins = 95 mins

95 mins = 1 h 35 mins

40 mins and 55 mins add up to more than 60 mins. Regroup the result!

Then add the hours.
1 h 35 mins + 1 h = 2 h 35 mins

She waited for 2 h 35 mins altogether.

4 2 h 45 mins + 5 h 35 mins = ?

First add the minutes.
45 mins + 35 mins = ☐ mins

☐ mins = ☐ h ☐ mins

Then add the hours.
2 h + 5 h + ☐ h ☐ mins = ☐ h ☐ mins

5 Add.
 a 3 h 40 mins + 5 h 25 mins **b** 4 h 55 mins + 6 h 15 mins

Home Maths Discuss the methods of adding up time with your child. Use the method shown in ① on page 99 when the minutes add up to less than 60. Use the method shown in ③ on page 100 when the minutes add up to more than 60.

Game

6 **Time shuffle!**

How to play:

Players: 2

You will need:
- a counter
- game board

1 Player 1 flicks a counter until it lands on a clock picture on the game board.

2 Player 1 gets the time value that is shown on the clock picture.
For example, they get the value 50 mins if the counter lands on the clock picture showing 50 mins.

3 Player 1 flicks the counter again to get another time value. For example, if they get the value 2 h, they add up the two time values:
50 mins + 2 h = 2 h 50 mins

4 Player 2 checks the answer.
Player 1 gets 1 point if their answer is correct.

The player with the higher score wins!

5 Take turns to play.
Play five rounds each.

Practice Book 3D, p.11

101

Let's Learn!

Subtraction

1 Ruby's dad took 2 h 15 mins to paint his bedroom.
Then he took 1 h 5 mins to paint his dining room.
How much longer did he take to paint the bedroom than the dining room?

2 h 15 mins – 1 h 5 mins = ?

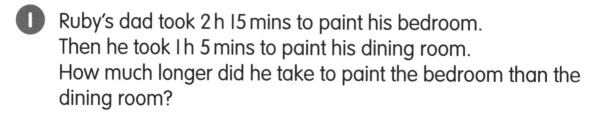

First subtract the hours.

2 h – 1 h 1 h

Then subtract the minutes.

15 mins – 5 mins 10 mins

2 h 15 mins – 1 h 5 mins = 1 h 10 mins

He took 1 h 10 mins longer to paint the bedroom than the dining room.

2 8 h 45 mins – 3 h 20 mins = ?

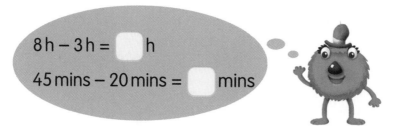

8 h – 3 h = ☐ h

45 mins – 20 mins = ☐ mins

8 h 45 mins – 3 h 20 mins = ☐ h ☐ mins

3 Omar cycled for 4 h 30 mins.
Jack cycled for 2 h 50 mins.
How much longer did Omar
cycle for than Jack?

4 h 30 mins – 2 h 50 mins = ?

First regroup 4 h 30 mins.
4 h 30 mins = 3 h 90 mins

You can't subtract
50 mins from 30 mins.
Regroup 4 h 30 mins!

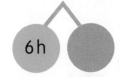

3 h   90 mins

Then subtract the times.
3 h 90 mins – 2 h 50 mins = 1 h 40 mins

Omar cycled for 1 h 40 mins longer than Jack.

4 7 h 20 mins – 4 h 45 mins = ?

First regroup 7 h 20 mins.
7 h 20 mins = 6 h ⬚ mins

6 h ⬚

Then subtract the times.

6 h ⬚ mins – 4 h ⬚ mins = ⬚ h ⬚ mins

5 Subtract.

a   4 h 30 mins – 2 h 45 mins   b   8 h 35 mins – 4 h 50 mins

Home Maths

Look at the methods of subtracting time with your child. Encourage them to use the method shown in ① on page 102 when you can subtract the minutes without regrouping. Use the method shown in ③ on page 103 when you can't subtract the minutes without regrouping.

Game

Players: 4

You will need:
- paper strips
- a bag

6 **Let's subtract!**

How to play:

1 Each player writes four subtraction questions on time. Write one question on each paper strip. An example of a subtraction question is:

2 h 15 mins – 1 h 20 mins = ⬭

2 Put all the questions into a bag.

3 Player 1 picks a question from the bag. They work out the answer.

2 h 15 mins – 1 h 20 mins = 55 mins

4 The other players check the answer. Player 1 gets 1 point if the answer is correct.

I got it right!

5 Take turns to play. Play four rounds each.

The player with the highest score wins!

Practice Book 3D, p.13

Let's Learn!

Duration in hours and minutes

1 Farha's violin lesson started at 3:00 p.m.
It ended at 5:00 p.m.
How long was her violin lesson?

Start:

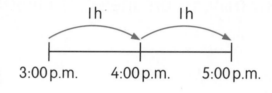

3:00 p.m.   4:00 p.m.   5:00 p.m.

End:

The lesson lasted 2 hours.

2 Ella started reading her book at 6:45 p.m.
She finished at 7:20 p.m.
How long did she spend reading?

Start:

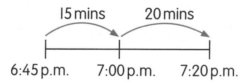

6:45 p.m.   7:00 p.m.   7:20 p.m.

End:

15 mins + 20 mins = 35 mins

Ella spent 35 minutes reading.

3 **a** What time is 3 hours after 7:00 p.m.?

b What time is 2 hours after 7:15 p.m.?

c How many hours are there from 9:00 a.m. to midday?

d How many hours are there from 2:30 p.m. to 4:30 p.m.?

e What time is 15 minutes after 11:00 a.m.?

f What time is 45 minutes after 11:30 a.m.?

g How many minutes are there from 4:00 p.m. to 4:35 p.m.?

h How many minutes are there from 11:50 a.m. to 12:25 p.m.?

4 Miya and her mum watched
a TV programme.
The programme started at
7:50 a.m. and ended at 9:15 a.m.
How long did the programme last?

Start: 7:50 a.m.
or 10 minutes to 8

End: 9:15 a.m.
or 15 minutes past 9

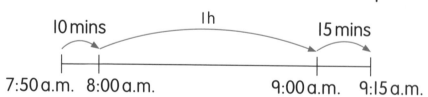

10 mins + 1h + 15 mins   or   10 mins + 15 mins = 25 mins
= 1h 25 mins   1h + 25 mins = 1h 25 mins

The programme lasted 1h 25 mins.

5 Ruby had a birthday party.

Look at the clocks below.
What time did the party start?
What time did the party end?
Use **past** or **to**.

Start: 25 minutes ⬜ 6
or 5:35 p.m.

End: 20 minutes ⬜ 8
or 8:20 p.m.

How long was the party?

⬜ mins   ⬜ h   ⬜ mins

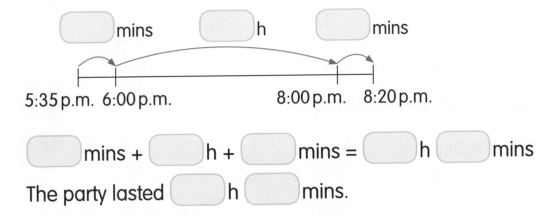

5:35 p.m. 6:00 p.m.   8:00 p.m.   8:20 p.m.

⬜ mins + ⬜ h + ⬜ mins = ⬜ h ⬜ mins

The party lasted ⬜ h ⬜ mins.

6 Omar's dad did a puzzle.
He started at 10:30 p.m. and finished it in 1 h 45 mins.
What time did he finish doing the puzzle?

At midnight p.m. becomes a.m.

Count forwards.

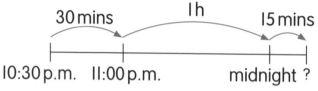

30 mins   1 h   15 mins

10:30 p.m.   11:00 p.m.   midnight ?

Check:
1 hour before 12:15 a.m. is 11:15 p.m.
45 minutes before 11:15 p.m. is 10:30 p.m.

30 minutes after 10:30 p.m. is 11:00 p.m.
1 hour after 11:00 p.m. is midnight.
15 minutes after midnight is 12:15 a.m.

Omar's dad finished doing the puzzle at 12:15 a.m.

7 Ella baked some biscuits for a school fair.
She took 2 h 35 mins to make the biscuits.
She started making them at 10:10 a.m.
When did she finish making them?

1 h   1 h   35 mins

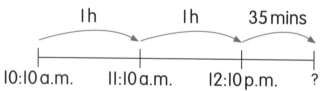

10:10 a.m.   11:10 a.m.   12:10 p.m.   ?

2 hours after 10:10 a.m. is 12:10 p.m.

35 minutes after 12:10 p.m. is ⬚

She finished making them at ⬚

At midday a.m. becomes p.m.

8 Ella packed the biscuits into bags.
She finished packing them at 3 p.m.
She took 1 h 50 mins to pack them.
When did she begin packing them?

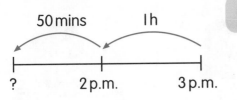

50 mins   1 h

?   2 p.m.   3 p.m.

Count back!

1 hour before 3 p.m. is 2 p.m.
50 minutes before 2 p.m. is 1:10 p.m.

Ella began packing them at 1:10 p.m.

Check:
50 minutes after 1:10 p.m.
is 2 p.m.
1 hour after 2 p.m. is 3 p.m.

9 Peter's mum spent 45 minutes reading her book.
She finished her book at 12:05 a.m.
What time did she start reading her book?

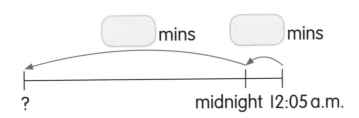

( ) mins   ( ) mins

?   midnight 12:05 a.m.

Peter's mum started reading her book at ( )

Activity

10 **1** Work in groups of four.
Take turns to tell one another the time you start and end each activity below.

Travelling to school

Playing a game

Having lunch

2 Write down your start time and end time for each activity.

Example

Having lunch: Start time = 1:20 p.m.
                  End time = 1:55 p.m.

3 Draw the timeline of each activity. Then find the duration.

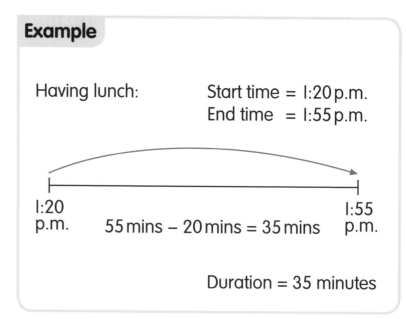

1:20 p.m.   55 mins – 20 mins = 35 mins   1:55 p.m.

Duration = 35 minutes

4 Answer these questions.

a Who takes the longest time to travel to school?

b Who takes the shortest time to have lunch?

c Who takes the shortest time to play a game?

Practice Book 3D, p.15

Let's Learn!

Word problems

1 Mr Magical is a magician.
He spends 45 minutes performing each show.
He is paid £90 an hour.
On Saturday he performed 8 shows.

    a How many hours did Mr Magical spend performing
8 shows?

    b How much did Mr Magical earn performing 8 shows?

    a 1 show → 45 mins
       8 shows → 8 × 45 mins
             = 360 mins
             = 6 h

$$\begin{array}{r} 4\,5 \\ \times\quad 8 \\ \hline 3\,6\,0 \\ {}_{4} \end{array}$$

> 1 h = 60 mins
> 6 h = 6 × 60 mins
> Think of the 6 times table:
> 6 × 6 = 36
> 6 × 60 = 360

Mr Magical spent 6 hours performing 8 shows.

    b 1 hour → £90
       6 hours → 6 × £90
            = £540

> 6 × 9 = 54
> 6 × 90 = 540

Mr Magical earned £540 for performing
8 shows.

2 Millie's aunt works as a fitness instructor.
She is paid £35 an hour.
The chart shows the days she works
each week and the number of hours
she works on each day.

Works on	Mon	Wed	Fri
Number of hours	2h	3h	2h

a How many hours does Millie's aunt work in a week?

b How much does Millie's aunt earn in a week?

a ⬭ ⬭ ⬭ ⬭ = ⬭

Millie's aunt works ⬭ hours in a week.

b I hour → £⬭

⬭ hours → ⬭ ⬭ £⬭ = £⬭

Millie's aunt earns £⬭ in a week.

3 Liam spent I h 40 mins doing his homework.
Then he spent another 45 minutes practising the piano.
He finished his homework and piano practice at 5:30 p.m.
What time did he begin doing his homework?

⬭ ⬭ ⬭ = ⬭

He spent ⬭ h ⬭ mins on
his homework and piano practice.

⬭ h ⬭ mins

First find the total
time Liam spent on
his homework and
piano practice.

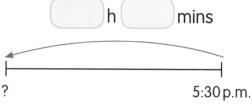

?   5:30 p.m.

Liam began doing his homework at ⬭ p.m.

4 Mrs Williams arrived at a train station.
Her watch showed the time as 6:45 a.m.
Her watch was 20 minutes slow.

a What was the actual time shown on the train station's clock?

b The train arrived 10 minutes later.
What time did the train arrive according to the train
station's clock?

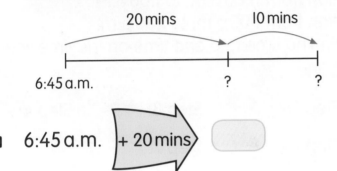

a 6:45 a.m. + 20 mins ⟶ ⬭

The actual time shown on the train station's clock was ⬭

b ⬭ a.m. 10 mins later ⟶ ⬭

According to the train station's clock, the train arrived at the
train station at ⬭

Practice Book 3D, p.19

Maths Journal

5 The steps for finding the duration from 10:20 a.m. to 1:30 p.m. are not in order. Put them in the correct order:

a Find the duration from 10:20 a.m. to 11:00 a.m.
b Mark the hours between the two end points.
c Add the durations.
d Find the duration from 11:00 a.m. to 1:00 p.m.
e Find the duration from 1:00 p.m. to 1:30 p.m.
f Mark the beginning time and end time on the time line.
g Draw the time line.

Step 1: g   Step 2: f   Step 3: b   Step 4: a

Step 5: d   Step 6: e   Step 7: c

Find the duration from 1:15 p.m. to 11:20 p.m.
Say whether the steps are the same as above and rewrite the steps that are different.

Step 1: ___   Step 2: ___   Step 3: ___   Step 4: ___

Step 5: ___   Step 6: ___   Step 7: ___

Put On Your Thinking Caps!

6 Ross takes a flight from Manchester to Athens at 8:15 a.m.
The journey takes 3 h 40 mins.
There are flights from Athens to Manchester every 3 hours from 8:15 a.m.
Ross wants to return to Manchester on the same day.
What is the latest flight that he can take?

Practice Book 3D, p.25   Practice Book 3D, p.26

Let's Learn!

Understanding angles

1 Jack made an angle using his arm.

An angle is the amount of turning between two lines at a point.

2 Here are some straws placed in pairs.

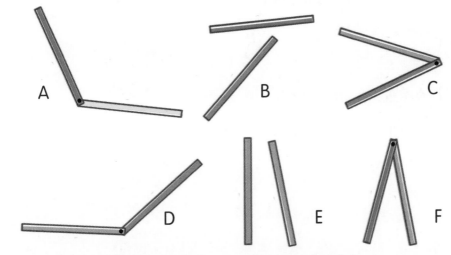

A B C

D E F

a Which of these pairs make angles?

b Which of these pairs do not make angles?

3 Tai is making a greater angle than the angle Jack is making.

Tai   Jack

4 Here are some angles made with lolly sticks.

 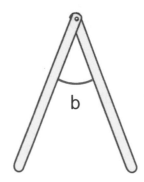

a Which angle is smaller?

b Which angle is greater?

Activity

5

1   Work in pairs. You will need a sheet of drawing paper, split pins, glue and some paper strips labelled 1 and 2.

2   Using one set of strips, stick Strip 2 onto the drawing paper as shown. Fasten Strip 1 onto Strip 2 so that only Strip 1 can move.

3   Make a few more sets of strips like the one made in **2**.

4   Using one set of strips, turn Strip 1 to make an angle as shown below.

       Name it Angle a.

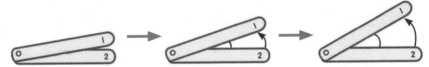

5   Using a second set of strips, make an angle smaller than Angle a. Call it Angle b.
Tell your partner how you know this angle is smaller than Angle a.

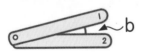

6   Using a third set of strips, make an angle greater than Angle a. Call it Angle c.
Tell your partner how you know this angle is greater than Angle a.

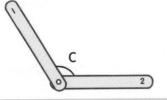

6 Draw some different angles on a piece of paper and show them to your friends.

7 Look at the angles below made using straws.

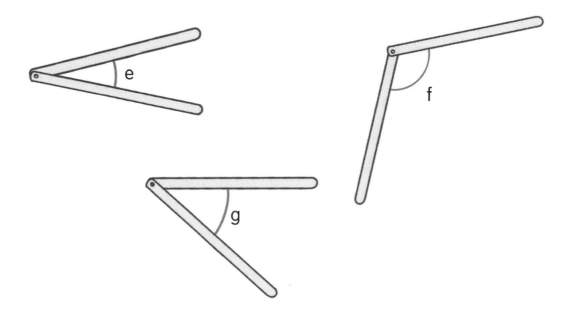

a Which angle is the smallest?

b Which angle is the greatest?

c Arrange the angles in order.
Begin with the smallest.

8 Arrange the following angles in order.
Begin with the greatest.

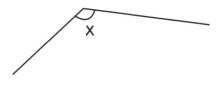

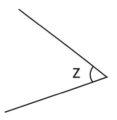

Practice Book 3D, p.27

Let's Learn!

Identifying angles

1 Look at the square shape and the triangle shape below.

The square shape has four angles.
The triangle shape has three angles.

In a shape, each angle is made by two straight lines meeting at a point.

2 Now look at these two shapes.

Copy these shapes. Mark all the angles inside the shapes.

3 Here are some examples of angles found on objects.

Can you find more angles around you?

In an object, each angle is made by two straight sides meeting at a point.

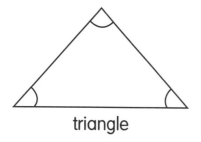

triangle

A triangle has three sides and three angles.

A rectangle has four sides and four angles. How many sides and angles does a square have?

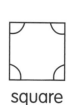

rectangle   square

5

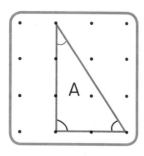
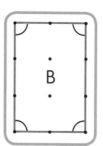

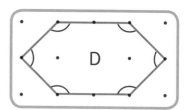

How many sides and angles does each shape have?

a Shape A has [ ] sides and [ ] angles.

b Shape B has [ ] sides and [ ] angles.

c Shape C has [ ] sides and [ ] angles.

d Shape D has [ ] sides and [ ] angles.

What do you notice about the number of sides and the number of angles for each shape?

Activity

6 Work in pairs.
You will need some drawing paper, some coloured pencils, a ruler and a worksheet.

I Draw the following:

a a 3-sided shape.

b a 4-sided shape.

c a 5-sided shape.

d a 6-sided shape.

2 Mark and colour the angles inside each shape.

3 Complete the worksheet to show the number of angles in each shape.

Angle Worksheet

Type of Shape	Number of Angles
3-sided	
4-sided	
5-sided	
6-sided	

Practice Book 3D, p.31

Let's Explore!

7 You will need a geoboard and some rubber bands or some square dotty paper.

1 Make triangles using the geoboard or square dotty paper. An example is shown below.

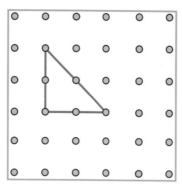

> The triangles must look different from one another.

a How many different triangles can you make? In what ways are they different?

b How many sides does each triangle have?

c How many angles does each triangle have?

d What can you say about the number of sides and the number of angles in a triangle?

2 Make rectangles using the geoboard or the square dotty paper.

> The rectangles must look different from one another.

a How many different rectangles can you make? In what ways are they different?

b How many sides does each rectangle have?

c How many angles does each rectangle have?

d What can you say about the number of sides and the number of angles in a rectangle?

Let's Learn!

Right angles

1 Ella folded a sheet of paper twice to make an angle like this:

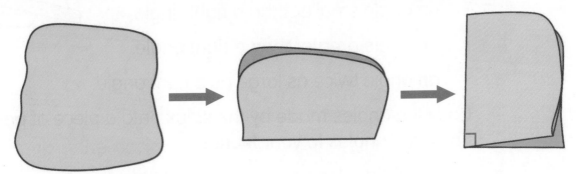

The angle Ella made is a **right angle**.

2 We can check for a right angle and mark it as shown.

The symbol for a right angle is ⌐.

3 Which of these angles is equal to a right angle?
Use 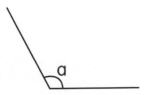 to find out.

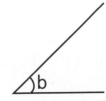

Angle a is greater than a right angle.

Angle b is smaller than a right angle.

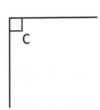

Angle c is equal to a right angle.

Activity

4   a   Make a set of strips for making angles as shown on page 117. Use the strips to make:

- a right angle.

- an angle smaller than a right angle.

- an angle greater than a right angle.

- an angle twice as large as a right angle.

Copy the angles made by the strips onto a piece of paper. Show the angles to your friends.

   b   Draw right angles on a piece of paper.
First draw a straight line.

Then draw a second straight line to join the first line like this:

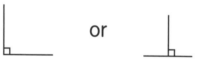

You have made a right angle.

5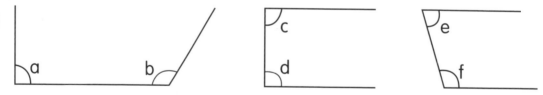

Make a and use it to answer these questions about the angles above.

   a   Which angles are right angles?

   b   Which angles are greater than a right angle?

   c   Which angle is smaller than a right angle?

6 This is a square.

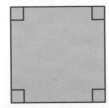

There are four right angles in a square.

7 How many right angles are there in each shape?

Use to help you find out.

a
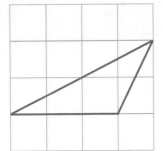

b
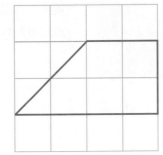

c
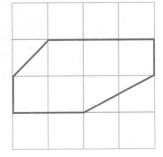

Activity

8 Use a rubber band and a geoboard to make the following shapes. Then draw the shapes on squared paper.

  a A shape which has a right angle, two angles smaller than a right angle and one angle greater than a right angle.

  b A shape which has a right angle, two angles greater than a right angle and one angle smaller than a right angle.

  c Make your own shape with seven sides and at least one right angle.
  How many angles are greater than a right angle?
  How many angles are smaller than a right angle?
  How many angles are right angles?

Practice Book 3D, p.35

Put On Your Thinking Caps!

9 Trace the tangram below and cut out the seven pieces.

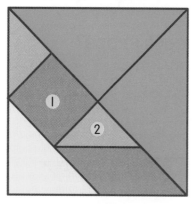

A tangram is a Chinese puzzle made up of seven pieces which can be pieced into a square.

a The shape below is made up of two tangram pieces. It has two right angles, one angle smaller than a right angle and one angle greater than a right angle.

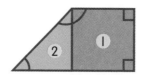

Make two more shapes which have two right angles, one angle smaller than a right angle and one angle greater than a right angle each, using:

| three tangram pieces | four tangram pieces |

b Arrange six pieces of the tangram to make a shape which has three right angles and two angles greater than a right angle.

Practice Book 3D, p.37 ▶   Practice Book 3D, p.38 ▶

Perpendicular and Parallel Lines

Let's Learn!

Perpendicular lines

1 When a sheet of paper is folded twice as shown below, the angle made is a right angle.

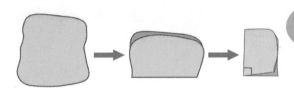

Do you remember? What is a right angle?

The corner of a ruler is also a right angle.

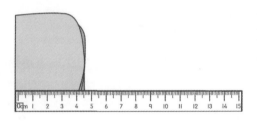

We can use a folded piece of paper or a ruler to check for right angles.

2 The lines shown below are **perpendicular lines**.

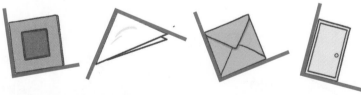

Perpendicular lines can be found on things around us.

What are perpendicular lines?

Perpendicular lines are two straight lines that meet at a right angle.

3 Here are some lines drawn on square grid paper.

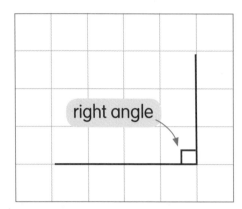

right angle

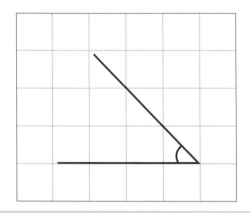

These two lines are perpendicular lines.
They meet at a right angle.

These two lines are not perpendicular lines.
They do not meet at a right angle.

4

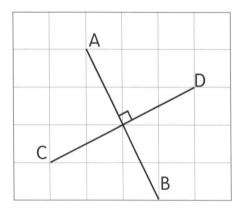

AB and CD cross at right angles.
AB **is perpendicular to** CD.

We write: AB ⊥ CD

⊥ stands for **is perpendicular to**.

5

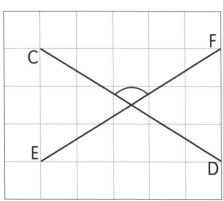

Is CD ⊥ EF?

No.
The lines do not cross at right angles.

6 How can we check whether the two pairs of lines are perpendicular lines?

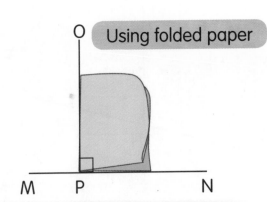

Using folded paper

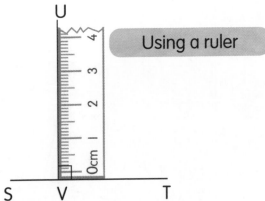

Using a ruler

Put the folded paper against the two lines as shown.
The lines meet at a right angle.
OP is perpendicular to MN.
OP ⊥ MN

Put a ruler against the two lines as shown.
The lines meet at a right angle.
UV is perpendicular to ST.
UV ⊥ ST

7 **a** Is GH ⊥ HI?

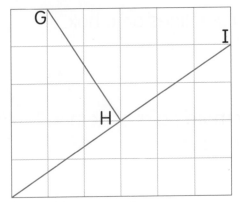

b Is PQ ⊥ QR?

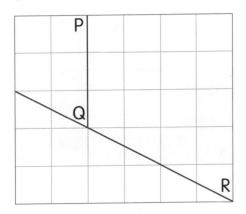

c Is ST ⊥ TU?

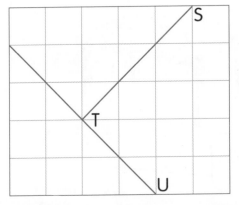

d Is XY ⊥ YZ?

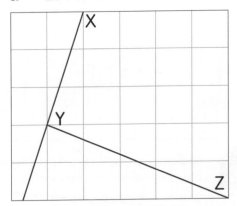

8 Which line is perpendicular to AB?

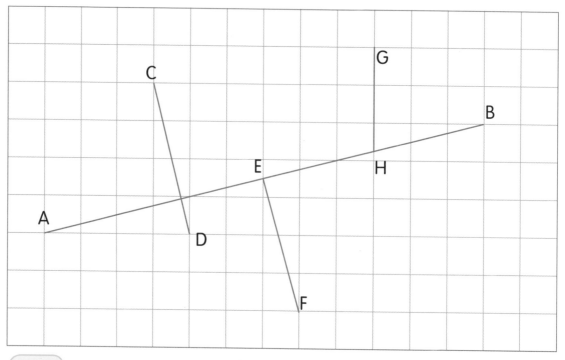

[blank] is perpendicular to AB.

9 Here are some pairs of perpendicular lines on a box.

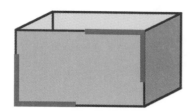

How many more pairs of perpendicular lines can you find?

10 Can you find pairs of perpendicular lines on the objects below?

£10

Activity

11 **a** Work in pairs.

1 Look around your classroom and school.

2 Find things with perpendicular lines and things with no perpendicular lines.

3 Check the lines with your folded paper or ruler.

4 Copy the charts shown below into your book. Record the things and the places in the charts.

5 Compare your things with those found by your classmates.

Things with Perpendicular Lines	Places Where I Found these Things
bench	school hall

Things with No Perpendicular Lines	Places Where I Found these Things
branches of plants	school garden

Optional activity:
Take photographs of the things you found in **a**.

Make copies of the photographs and display them in your classroom.

b Think of some other objects that are not in the classroom. Draw them on a piece of paper.
Check if there are any perpendicular lines in the objects by using a ruler.

Practice Book 3D, p.39

Let's Learn!

Drawing perpendicular lines

1 You can draw various types of perpendicular lines on square grid paper.

a Draw a line along any line on square grid paper.

The line must lie along the grid and pass through at least two points on the grid where the grid lines cross.

Name it AB.

Use a ruler to help you draw.

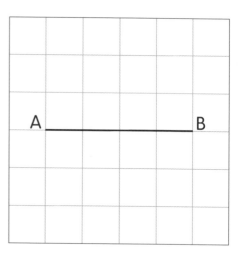

Draw two lines to meet AB as shown.

Name the lines CD and EF.

They are drawn in a different direction to AB.

Each line must lie along the grid and pass through at least two points on the grid where the grid lines cross.

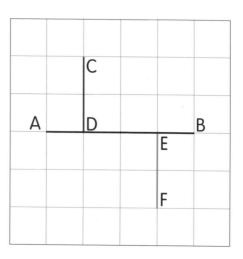

Lines CD and EF are perpendicular to AB.

b Draw a line as shown on the right.

The line must pass through at least two points on the grid where the grid lines cross.

Name it GH.

The end points G and H of the line are at opposite corners of a big square made up of 4 unit squares.

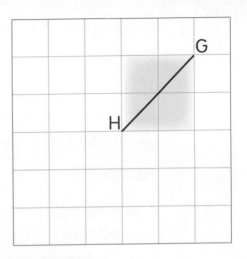

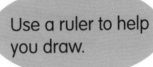

Use a ruler to help you draw.

At point H, draw lines KH and LH as shown.

The end points of lines KH and LH are at opposite corners of big squares. Each big square is made up of 4 unit squares.

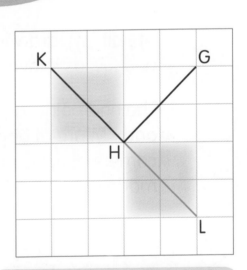

You have drawn two lines perpendicular to GH!

Use your ruler to check that the lines meet at right angles.

KH ⊥ HG and LH ⊥ HG.

c Draw a line as shown on the right.

The line must pass through at least two points on the grid where the grid lines cross.

Name it MN.

The end points M and N of the line MN are at opposite corners of a rectangle made up of 2 unit squares.

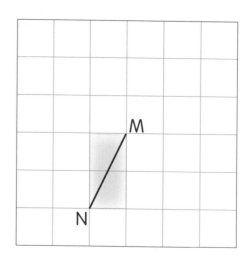

Use a ruler to help you draw.

At point M, draw lines QM and RM as shown.

The end points of lines QM and RM are at opposite corners of rectangles each made up of 2 unit squares.

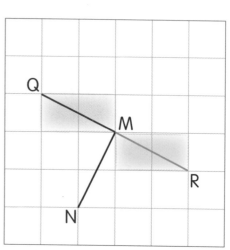

You have drawn two lines perpendicular to MN!

Use your ruler to check that the lines meet at right angles.

QM ⊥ MN and RM ⊥ MN.

2

Copy the lines given below onto another sheet of square grid paper. For each line, draw a line perpendicular to it.

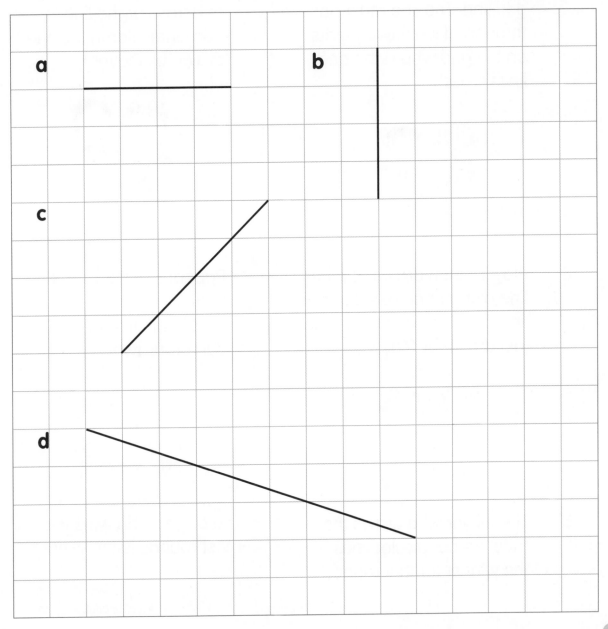

a

b

c

d

Game

3 How to play:

Players: 2
You will need:
- square grid paper
- coloured pencils
- rulers

1 Player 1 draws a line of any length along or across a grid line. The line must pass through at least two points on the grid where the grid lines cross.

2 Player 2 draws a line in a different colour along or across a grid line perpendicular to the line drawn by Player 1.

3 Player 1 then draws another line along or across a grid line perpendicular to the line just drawn by Player 2.

4 Repeat steps **2** and **3** until no more perpendicular lines can be drawn.

5 The player who draws the most perpendicular lines is the winner for that round.

The player who wins the most rounds is the winner.

Practice Book 3D, p.43

Let's Explore!

4 **a** Look at the pair of perpendicular lines drawn on the square grid paper below.
Look at how this pair of perpendicular lines is drawn.

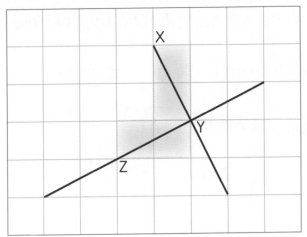

The points XY and YZ of each line are at opposite corners of rectangles each made up of 2 unit squares.

On a sheet of square grid paper, draw a few more pairs of perpendicular lines. Use the following rules:

Each line must be drawn across at least two points on the square grid paper.

Each line must be a different length.

b Can you think of other ways of drawing perpendicular lines?
Draw them on a sheet of square grid paper.
Check that the lines are perpendicular with your ruler.

Let's Learn!

Parallel lines

1 AB and CD are a pair of **parallel lines**.
These two straight lines will not meet no matter how long you draw them.
The distance between them is always the same.

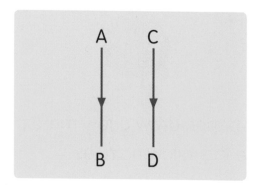

2

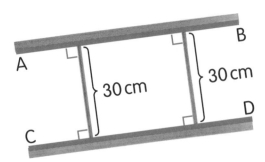

AB and CD are parallel lines.
We write: AB // CD

EF and GH are parallel lines.
We write: EF // GH

// stands for **is parallel to**.
We mark arrowheads to show lines are parallel.

3 Parallel lines can be found on things around us.

4 Here are some sets of lines drawn on square grid paper.
How can you tell if the lines are parallel?

a

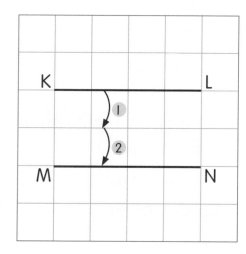

KL and MN are parallel lines. You can use a ruler and draw them like this from left to right.

What is the distance between the lines?

Count the number of unit squares between the lines.

KL is always 2 unit squares from MN.
KL // MN.

b

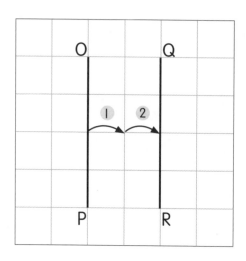

OP and QR are parallel lines. You can use a ruler and draw them straight down like this.

OP is always 2 unit squares from QR.

c

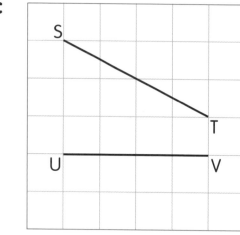

Are ST and UV always the same distance apart?

No.

Point S is 3 unit squares away from point U.

Point T is 1 unit square away from point V.

ST and UV are not parallel to each other.

5 Are ST and MN parallel lines?

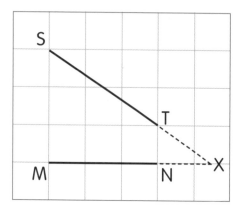

No. If you make ST and MN longer by drawing the dotted lines as shown, they will meet at a point X.

The distance between the lines is not the same.

6 These are lines drawn on square grid paper.
Which pairs of lines are parallel?

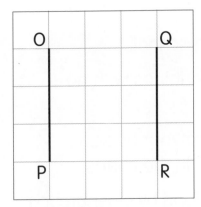
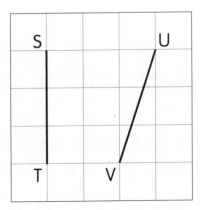
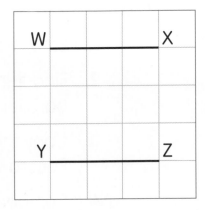

7 Copy these shapes onto square grid paper.
Name the pairs of parallel lines in each shape.

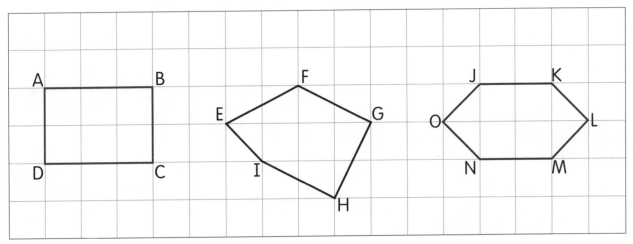

8 Can you find pairs of parallel lines on the objects below?

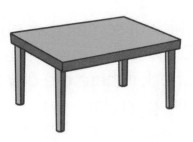

Activity

9 **a** Work in pairs.

1 Look around your classroom and school.

2 Find things with parallel lines and things with no parallel lines.

3 Copy the charts shown below into your book. Record the things and the places in the charts.

4 Compare your things with those found by other groups.

Things with Parallel Lines	Places Where I Found these Things
tables	classroom

Things with No Parallel Lines	Places Where I Found these Things
footballs	school hall

Optional activity:
Take photographs of the things you found in **a**.
Make copies of the photographs and display them in your classroom.

b Think of some other objects that are not in the classroom. Draw them on a piece of paper.
Check if there are any parallel lines in the objects by using a ruler.

Practice Book 3D, p.45

Let's Learn!

Drawing parallel lines

1 You can draw various types of parallel lines on square grid paper.

a Draw a line straight down along any line on the square grid paper.
The line must lie along the grid and pass through at least two points on the grid where the grid lines cross.

Name it AB.

> Use a ruler to help you draw!

Draw two other lines as shown.

Name the lines CD and EF.

What is the distance between the lines?

> Count the number of unit squares between the lines.

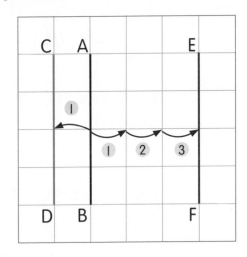

CD is always 1 unit square from AB.
EF is always 3 unit squares from AB.

AB // CD, AB // EF and CD // EF.

b Draw a line from left to right along any line on the square grid.

The line must lie along the grid and pass through at least two points on the grid where the grid lines cross.

Name it GH.

Use a ruler to help you draw!

Draw two other lines as shown.

Name the lines MN and KL.

Look at the distance between the lines.

MN is always 1 unit square from GH.

KL is always 3 unit squares from GH.

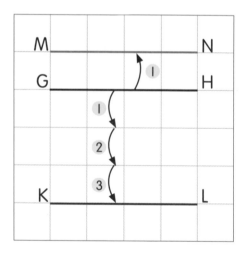

MN // GH, KL // GH and MN // KL.

c Draw a line as shown here.

The line must pass through at least two points on the grid where the grid lines cross.

Name it AB.

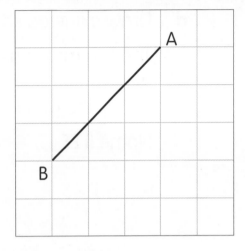

Use a ruler to help you draw!

Draw another line as shown here.

Name it CD.

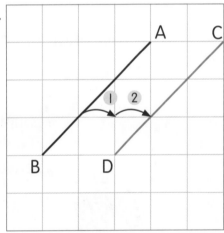

Count the number of unit squares between the lines.

Look at the distance between the points A and C and B and D.

The distances are equal.

AB // CD.

d Draw a line as shown here.

The line must pass through at least two points on the grid where the grid lines cross.

Name it EF.

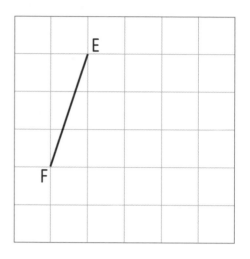

Use a ruler to help you draw!

Draw another line as shown here.

Name it GH.

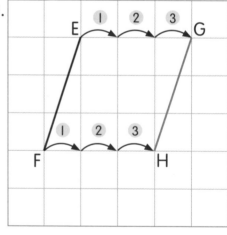

Count the number of unit squares between the lines.

Look at the distances between the points E and G and between points F and H.

The distances are equal.

EF // GH.

2 Copy the lines shown below onto a piece of square grid paper. For each line, draw a line parallel to it.

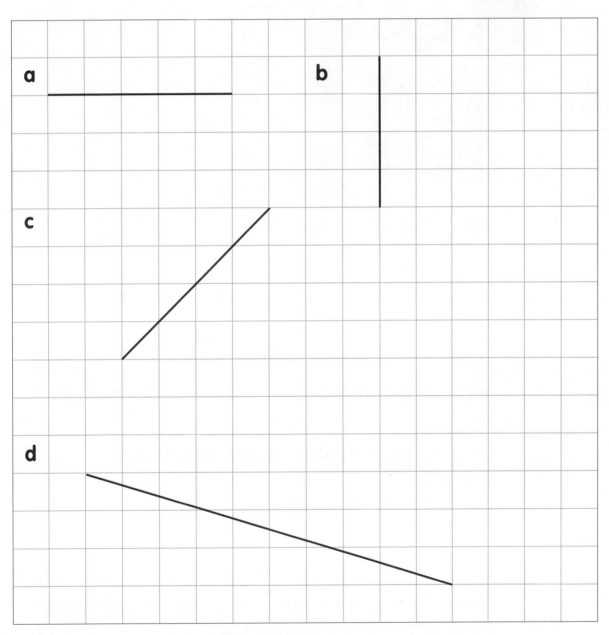

Home Maths — Use exercise books with square grid paper to practise drawing perpendicular and parallel lines with your child.

Practice Book 3D, p.49

147

Put On Your Thinking Caps!

3 **a**

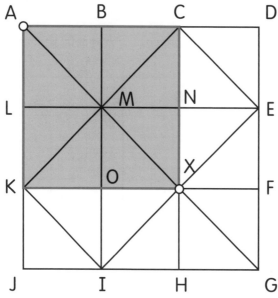

Name three pairs of perpendicular lines in the diagram.

You are standing at X. You want to go to A.
What is the shortest path to A?

Are there any lines perpendicular to the shortest path?
Name two.

Find three paths from X to A that are within the
shaded area.
Each path must be made up of one or more pairs of
perpendicular lines.

b Use five straws to make a diagram that has four pairs
of parallel lines and four pairs of perpendicular lines.
What does your diagram look like?

Practice Book 3D, p.51   Practice Book 3D, p.53

Unit 18 Area and Perimeter

Let's Learn!

Area

1 These shapes have been made using some square tiles.

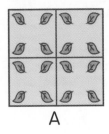 A

B

C

Count the number of square tiles in each shape.

Shape A is made up of 4 square tiles.
Shape B is made up of 5 square tiles.
Shape C is made up of 6 square tiles.

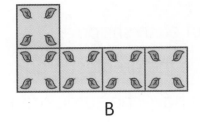

The amount of surface covered by the tiles is the **area** of each shape.

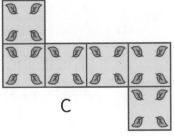

The area of Shape B is 5 tiles. What is the area of Shape A and Shape C?

Area is the amount of surface covered.

2 Here are some more shapes made using square tiles.

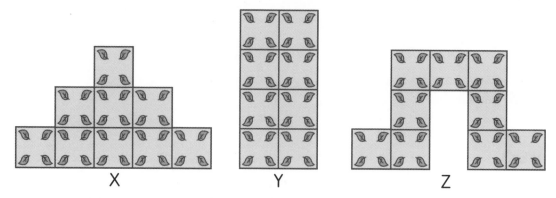

X   Y   Z

a How many square tiles make up each shape?

b What is the area of each shape?

Which shapes have the greatest area?

c Which two shapes have the same area?

3

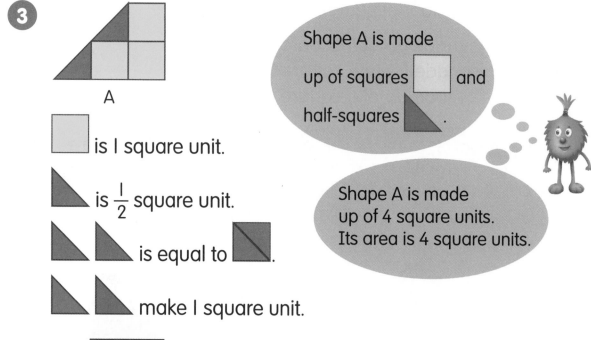

A

is I square unit.

is $\frac{1}{2}$ square unit.

is equal to ⬛.

make I square unit.

Shape A is made up of squares ⬜ and half-squares ◣.

Shape A is made up of 4 square units. Its area is 4 square units.

4

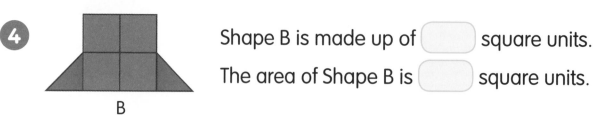

B

Shape B is made up of ⬜ square units.

The area of Shape B is ⬜ square units.

5 Find the area of each shape.
Give your answers in square units.

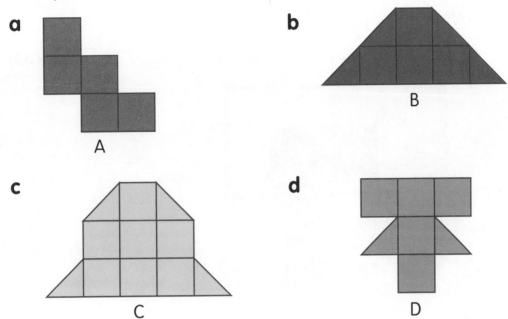

a

A

b

B

c

C

d

D

Which shape has the smallest area?

Which shape has the greatest area?

Which shapes have the same area?

6 **a** These shapes are made of tiles.
Which two shapes have the same area?

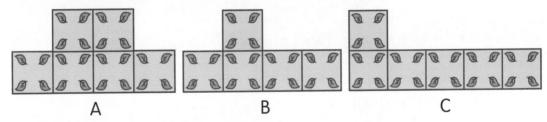

A   B   C

b You want all the shapes to have the same area.
Think of two ways of doing this.

Activity

7 **a** Work in groups of four.

Each group will need 10 squares and 10 half-squares.

Make four different shapes.
Use 4 squares and 2 half-squares for each shape.

The area of each shape is ⬚ square units.

Make four different shapes, each with the same area of 6 square units.
How many squares and half-squares did you use for each shape?

Design your own shape.

The shape is made up of ⬚ squares and ⬚ half-squares.

The area of the shape is ⬚ square units.

The shape represents a ⬚.

Activity

b Work in pairs.

Each pair will need 2 large sheets of paper.
Trace the red square and blue square and cut them out.
Make thirty red squares and twenty blue squares.

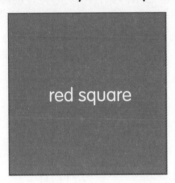

red square

blue square

Place red squares over the cover of your Maths book.
How many have you used? ⬚ red squares.

The area of the cover of the book is about ⬚ red squares.

Place blue squares over the cover of your Maths book.

How many have you used? ⬚ blue squares.

The area of the cover of the book is about ⬚ blue squares.

Practice Book 3D, p.55

Let's Explore!

8 You have nine triangle tiles. Use all the tiles to make three shapes.
Compare your shapes with those made by your classmates.
What do you notice about the areas of the shapes?

Let's Learn!

Square centimetres (cm²)

 1

This is a 1 cm square. Each side of the square is 1 cm long. Its area is 1 **square centimetre (cm²)**.

The **square centimetre (cm²)** is a unit of measurement for area.

1 cm
1 cm

A 2 cm square is made up of four 1 cm squares. Its area is 4 square centimetres (cm²).

1 cm
1 cm

a 2 cm square

2

1 cm
1 cm

a 3 cm square

Count the number of 1 cm squares!

A 3 cm square is made up of nine 1 cm squares.
The area of each 1 cm square is 1 cm².
The area of the 3 cm square is 9 cm².

 Home Maths   Explain to your child that 1 cm² is read as 1 square centimetre and not 1 centimetre square.

3

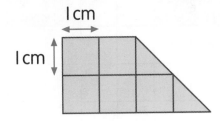

a 5 cm square

A 5 cm square is made up of

⬭ I cm squares.

The area of each I cm square is

⬭ cm².

The area of the 5 cm square

is ⬭ cm².

4 What is the area of this shape?

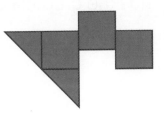

Activity

5 Draw the following shapes in your book and colour them in.

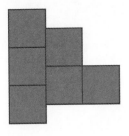

6 **a** Find the area of each shape.

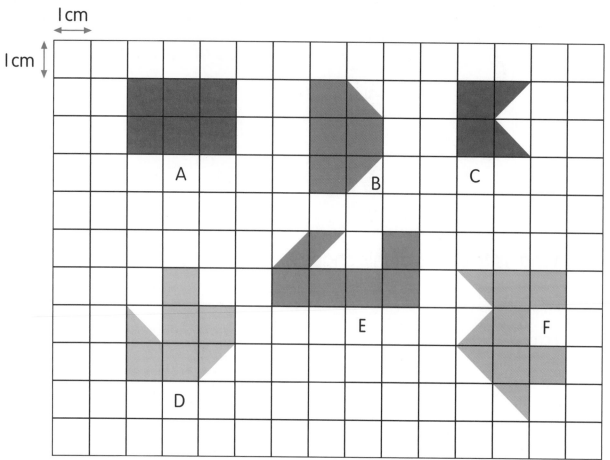

1 cm

1 cm

b Which shape has the smallest area?

c Which shape has the greatest area?

d Which shapes have the same area?

Home Maths Show your child what an actual 1 cm square looks like by drawing one using a ruler.

7 **a** What is the area of each shape?

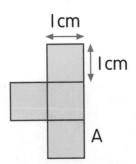

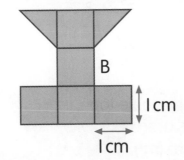

b Which shape has a greater area?

c You want both shapes to have the same area.
Think of two ways of doing this.

Practice Book 3D, p.59

Let's Explore!

8 How many I cm squares are there in each shape?

A

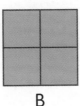

B

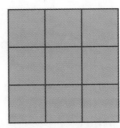

C

Shape	Number of squares
A	⬭ = I
B	⬭ = I + ⬭
C	⬭ = I + ⬭ + ⬭

Can you see a pattern?

Let's Learn!

Square metres (m²)

 Each side of this table top is 1 m long. Its area is 1 **square metre (m²)**.

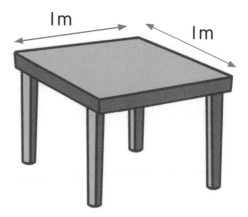

1 m   1 m

Which do you think is bigger, 1 cm² or 1 m²? Why?

The **square metre (m²)** is also a unit of measurement for area. 1 m² is bigger than 1 cm².

| Home Maths | Explain to your child that 1 m² is read as 1 square metre and not 1 metre square. |

2 A kitchen table is about 1 m².
The sticker has an area of 1 cm².

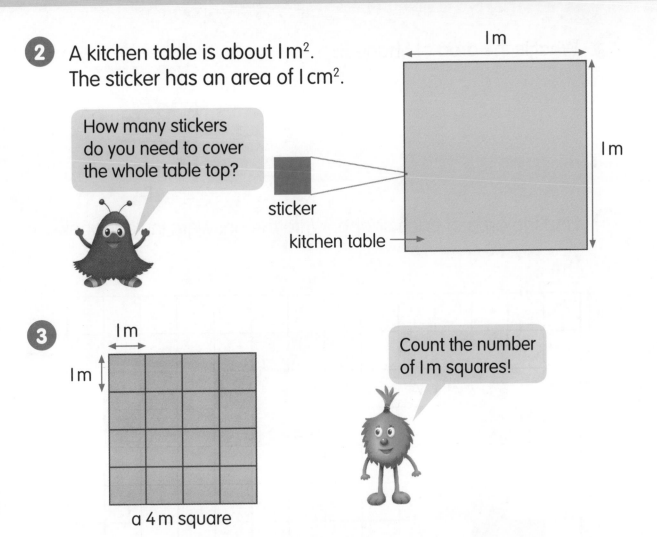

How many stickers do you need to cover the whole table top?

sticker

kitchen table

1 m

1 m

3

1 m

1 m

a 4 m square

Count the number of 1 m squares!

A 4 m square is made up of sixteen 1 m squares.
The area of each 1 m square is 1 m².
The area of the 4 m square is 16 m².

4

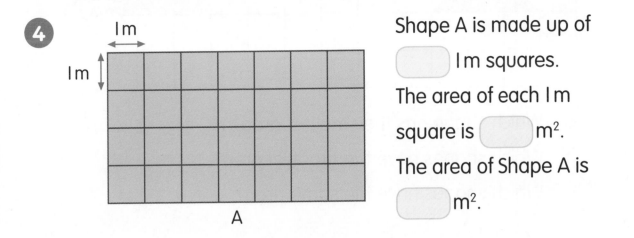

1 m

1 m

A

Shape A is made up of

⬜ 1 m squares.

The area of each 1 m

square is ⬜ m².

The area of Shape A is

⬜ m².

5 What is the area of Shape B?

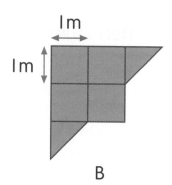

B

6 Find the area of each shape. Write the answers in your book.

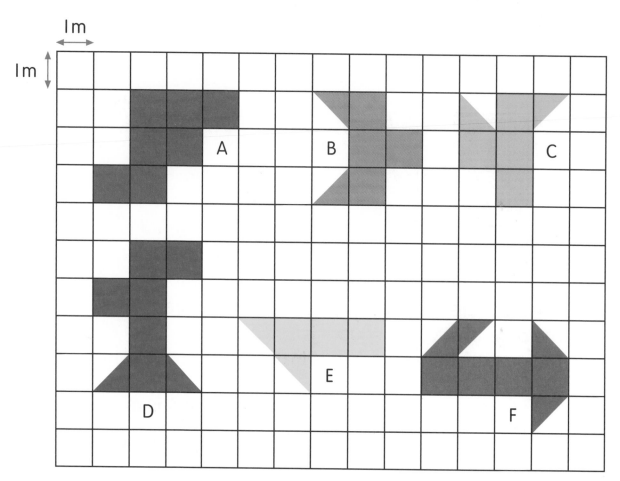

a Which shape has the smallest area?

b Which shapes have the greatest area?

c Which shapes have the same area?

Activity

7 **a** Look around your school and home.
Find things that have an area of about 1 cm² or 1 m².

Area	Things in School	Things at Home
About 1 cm²		
About 1 m²		

b Using pieces of wrapping paper and sticky tape, make a square piece of paper with an area of 1 m².
Using this piece of paper, estimate the area of the things in the chart below.

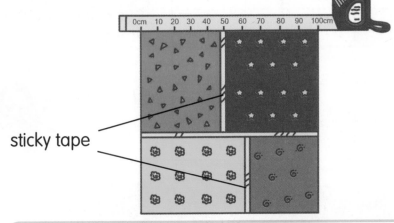

sticky tape

Things	Estimated Area
Cupboard door	
Canteen table	
Netball court	

Practice Book 3D, p.61

Home Maths Talk about the different sizes of things around your house. Show the difference between a 1 cm square and a 1 m square by drawing the 1 m square using a ruler or by mapping out the shape with some tape. Let your child see that a 1 m square is many times bigger than a 1 cm square.

Let's Explore!

8 You will need square grid paper.
Label a small square in the grid as 1 m².

Draw and colour as many different shapes as possible so that the area of each shape is 3 m².
Do not use half-squares.
Do not draw shapes that are the same and that you can get by turning.

Example

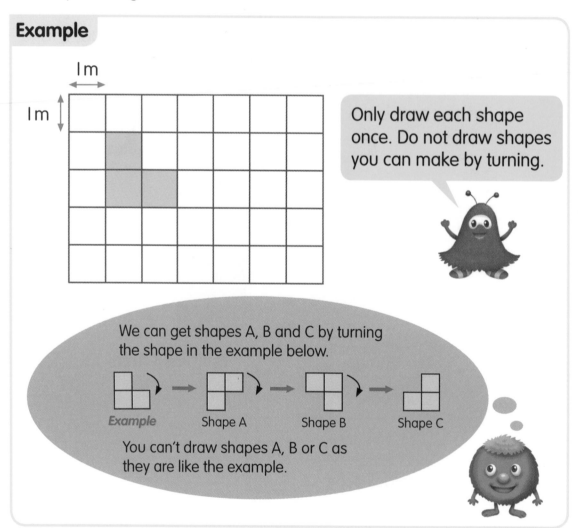

Only draw each shape once. Do not draw shapes you can make by turning.

We can get shapes A, B and C by turning the shape in the example below.

Example → Shape A → Shape B → Shape C

You can't draw shapes A, B or C as they are like the example.

How many more different shapes can you draw?

Let's Learn!

Perimeter and area

1 Ruby makes a rectangle with a rubber band on a geoboard.

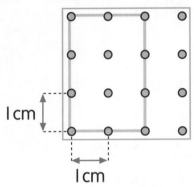

I cm

I cm

The **perimeter** of the rectangle is the distance around it.

The perimeter of the rectangle is 10 cm.
The area of the rectangle is 6 cm².

2

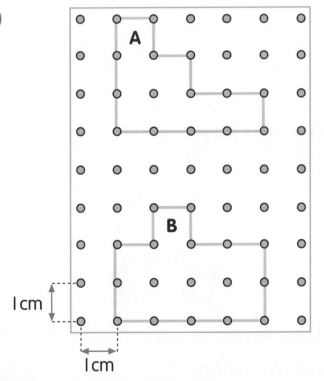

I cm

I cm

Miya makes two shapes on the geoboard.

They have the same perimeter.

The perimeter of each shape is ⬚ cm.

But they do not have the same area.

The area of Shape A is ⬚ cm².

The area of Shape B is ⬚ cm².

 Home Maths Ask your child to make shapes on a geoboard using string or a rubber band and encourage them to work out the areas and perimeters of these shapes.

Activity

3 Each group will need a geoboard and a rubber band, or squared paper.

Work in groups of four to do the following:

a Make this shape ▪. Then find the perimeter and area of the shape.

The perimeter of the shape is ⬚ cm.

The area of the shape is ⬚ cm².

b Make a shape with a perimeter of 8 cm. Then find its area.

The area of the shape is ⬚ cm².

4 These shapes are made up of 1 cm squares. Find the perimeter and area of each shape.

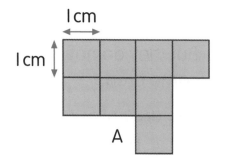

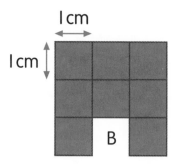

a Do Shapes A and B have the same area?

b Do they have the same perimeter?

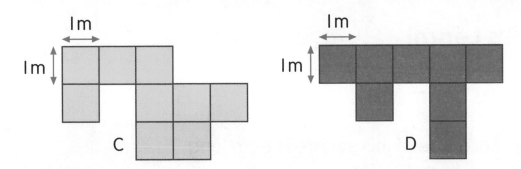

C

D

c Do Shapes C and D have the same area?

d Do they have the same perimeter?

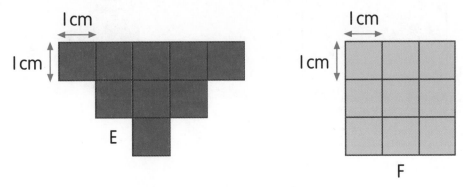

E

F

e Do Shapes E and F have the same area?

f Do they have the same perimeter?

Practice Book 3D, p.63

Let's Explore!

5 Work in groups of three or four.
Each group will need a geoboard and a rubber band,
or squared paper.
Make the following:

a Shapes that have an area of $8\,cm^2$.
Do the shapes have the same perimeter?

b Shapes that have a perimeter of 12 cm.
Do the shapes have the same area?

c A square with 4 cm sides.
What do you notice about its area and perimeter?

165

Let's Learn!

More perimeter

1 Each side of this square is 6 cm long.
Find its perimeter.

Perimeter = 6 + 6 + 6 + 6 = 24 cm

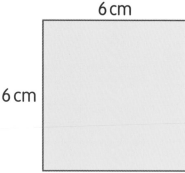

6 cm

6 cm

How many sides does
the square have?

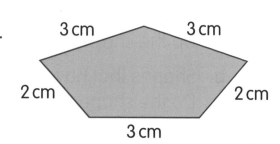

2 Find the perimeter of this rectangle.

Perimeter = ⬚ + ⬚ + ⬚ + ⬚

= ⬚ cm

9 cm

3 cm

3 Find the perimeter of this shape.

Perimeter = ⬚ cm

3 cm   3 cm

2 cm   2 cm

3 cm

4 Find the perimeter of each shape:

a

b

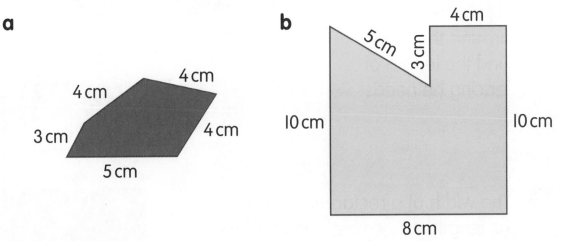

Activity

5 Here are some sticks with different lengths.

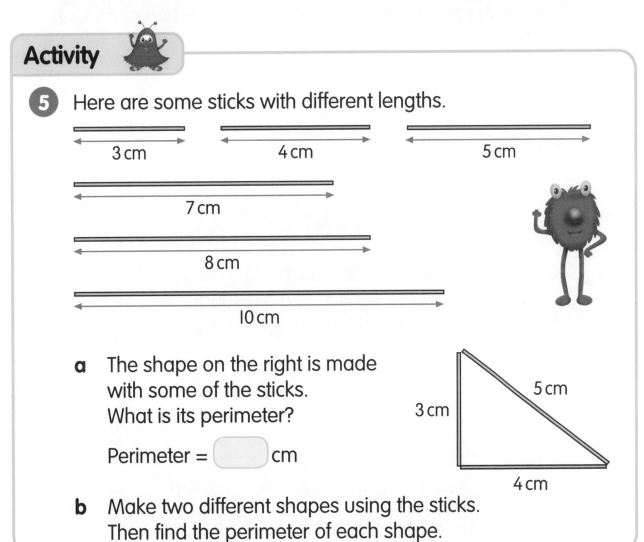

a The shape on the right is made with some of the sticks.
What is its perimeter?

Perimeter = ⬚ cm

b Make two different shapes using the sticks.
Then find the perimeter of each shape.

6 Mr Grey has a plot of land.
He wants to put a fence
around the land.
Find the length of
fencing he needs.

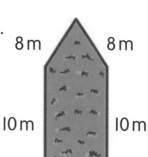

8 m   8 m

10 m   10 m

6 m

7 The width of a rectangle is 14 cm.
Its length is twice as long as its width.
What is the perimeter of the rectangle?

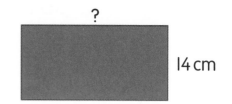

?

14 cm

Length = ⬭ × ⬭

= ⬭ cm

Perimeter = ⬭ + ⬭ + ⬭ + ⬭

= ⬭ cm

The perimeter of the rectangle is ⬭ cm.

8 Katie uses four square tiles, each with a 12 cm side, to
completely cover the surface of a big square tile.
What is the perimeter of the big square tile?

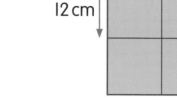

12 cm

12 cm

Length of one side of big square tile =

⬭ × ⬭ = ⬭ cm

Perimeter of big square tile =

⬭ + ⬭ + ⬭ + ⬭ = ⬭ cm

The perimeter of the big square tile is ⬭ cm.

Practice Book 3D, p.67

Let's Learn!

Area of a rectangle

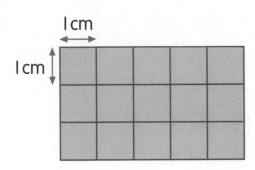

I cm

I cm

What is the area of this rectangle? Count the I cm squares covering the rectangle to find out.

There are 3 rows of I cm squares.
Each row has five I cm squares.
There are fifteen I cm squares covering the rectangle.
The area of the rectangle is 15 cm^2.

One side of the rectangle is called the **length**.
The perpendicular side is called the **width**.

length = 5 cm

width = 3 cm

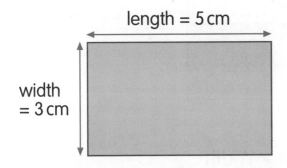

I know another way to find the area of the rectangle. I multiply the length by the width of the rectangle.

Area of rectangle = Length × Width

Area = 5 × 3 = 15 cm^2

2

1 cm

1 cm

A

Count the number of 1 cm squares covering Rectangle A.

There are ⬚ rows of 1 cm squares.

There are ⬚ 1 cm squares in each row.

There are ⬚ 1 cm squares covering Rectangle A.

The area of Rectangle A is ⬚ cm².

Do you remember the other way to find the area of a rectangle?

length = 8 cm

width = 2 cm

B

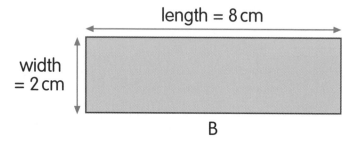

Area of Rectangle B = Length × Width

= ⬚ × ⬚

= ⬚ cm²

3 Square C is covered by I m squares.
Find the area of Square C using two different methods.

Method I

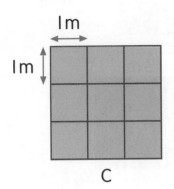

C

There are ⬭ rows of I m squares.

Each row has ⬭ I m squares.

There are ⬭ I m squares covering Square C.

The area of Square C is ⬭ m².

Method 2

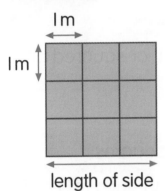

length of side

Area of Square C = $\frac{\text{Length}}{\text{of side}} \times \frac{\text{Length}}{\text{of side}}$

= ⬭ × ⬭

= ⬭ m²

The lengths of the sides of a square are the same.

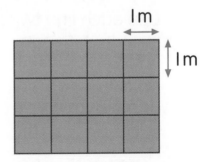

4 Find the area of each shape.

a

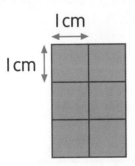

Area = Length × Width

= ⬭ × ⬭

= ⬭ cm²

b

Area = Length × Width

= ⬭ × ⬭

= ⬭ m²

5 Find the area of each shape.

a
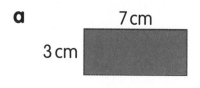
7 cm
3 cm

b
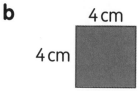
4 cm
4 cm

c
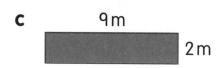
9 m
2 m

d
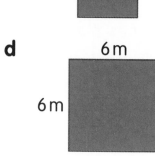
6 m
6 m

Activity

6 **a** Work in groups of four.

Use a geoboard and a rubber band, or squared paper to make four different rectangles.

For each rectangle:

- find the number of rows of I cm squares.

- find the number of I cm squares in each row.

- find the area using: Length × Width.

b Use these lines to make three different rectangles.
Use each line twice.
Now find the perimeter and area of each rectangle.

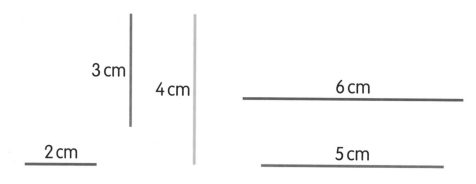

3 cm

4 cm

6 cm

2 cm

5 cm

7 cm

7 Farha's mum bent a 36 cm wire to make a square photo frame.
What is the area of the photo frame?

Length of one side =

$\boxed{} \div 4 = \boxed{}$

Area =

$\boxed{} \times \boxed{} = \boxed{}$

The area of the photo frame is $\boxed{}$ cm^2.

8 The length of one side of Thomas' square garden is 8 m.
He uses half of this garden for growing vegetables.
What area of his garden does he use for growing vegetables?

Method 1

8 m

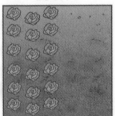

Half of length of one side of square garden =

$\boxed{} \div 2 = \boxed{}$

Area of garden for growing vegetables =

$\boxed{} \times \boxed{} = \boxed{}$

Method 2

Area of garden =

$\boxed{} \times 8 = \boxed{}$

Area of garden for growing vegetables =

$\boxed{} \div 2 = \boxed{}$

The area of his garden that Thomas uses for growing vegetables is

$\boxed{}$ m^2.

Practice Book 3D, p.71

Put On Your Thinking Caps!

9 **a** How many squares of different sizes can you make from the blue square below? The squares can overlap. Copy the chart and use it to help you find the answer.

Size of Square	Number of Squares
1 cm	
2 cm	
3 cm	
4 cm	

b Use a grid of square dotty paper as shown below. The grid must be 5 dots across by 3 dots down. How many squares and rectangles of different sizes can you draw on it?

The squares and rectangles can overlap.

Practice Book 3D, p.77 Practice Book 3D, p.79

Published by Marshall Cavendish Education
Times Centre, 1 New Industrial Road, Singapore 536196
Customer Service Hotline: (65) 6213 9444
Email: tmesales@mceducation.com
Website: www.mceducation.com

Distributed by
Oxford University Press
Great Clarendon Street, Oxford,
OX2 6DP, United Kingdom
www.oxfordprimary.co.uk
www.oxfordowl.co.uk

First published 2015
Reprinted 2015

ISBN 978-981-01-8879-5

Printed in China

Acknowledgements
Written by Dr Fong Ho Kheong, Chelvi Ramakrishnan and Michelle Choo

UK consultants: Carole Skinner, Simon d'Angelo and Elizabeth Gibbs

Cover artwork by Daron Parton

The authors and publisher would like to thank all schools and individuals
who helped to trial and review Inspire Maths resources.